Jobs Lost, Faith Found

Jobs Lost, Faith Found

A Spiritual Resource
for the Unemployed

Mary C. Lindberg

JOBS LOST, FAITH FOUND
A Spiritual Resource for the Unemployed

All biblical references in this book come from the New Revised Standard Version, unless otherwise noted.

Cover and interior design: Rob Dewey
Typesetting: PerfecType, Nashville, TN

Print ISBN: 978-1-5064-2739-3
eBook ISBN: 978-1-5064-3416-2

The paper used in this publication meets the minimum requirements of American National Standard for Information Sciences — Permanence of Paper for Printed Library Materials, ANSI Z329.48-1984.

Manufactured in the U.S.A.

Contents

Series Preface

MY MOST sincere wish is that the Living with Hope series will offer comfort, wisdom—and hope—to individuals facing life's most common and intimate challenges. Books in the series tackle complex problems such as addiction, parenting, unemployment, pregnancy loss, serious illness, trauma, and grief and encourage individuals, their families, and those who care for them. The series is bound together by a common message for those who are dealing with significant issues: you are not alone. There is hope.

This series offers first-person perspectives and insights from authors who know personally what it is like to face these struggles. As companions and guides, series contributors share personal experiences, offer valuable research from trusted experts, and suggest questions to help readers process their own responses and explore possible next steps. With empathy and honesty, these accessible volumes reassure individuals they are not alone in their pain, fear, or confusion.

The series is also a valuable resource for pastoral and spiritual care providers in faith-based settings. Parish pastors, lay ministers, chaplains, counselors, and other staff and volunteers can draw on these volumes to offer skilled and compassionate guidance to individuals in need of hope.

Each title in this series is offered with prayer for the reader's journey—one of discovery, further challenges, and transformation. You are not alone. There is hope.

Beth Ann Gaede, Series Editor

Titles in the Living with Hope Series

Nurturing Hope: Christian Pastoral Care in the Twenty-First Century
(Lynne M. Baab)

Dignity and Grace: Wisdom for Caregivers and Those Living with Dementia (Janet L. Ramsey)

Jobs Lost, Faith Found: A Spiritual Resource for the Unemployed
(Mary C. Lindberg)

They Don't Come with Instructions: Cries, Wisdom, and Hope for Parenting Children with Developmental Challenges
(Hollie M. Holt-Woehl)

True Connection: Using the NAME IT Model to Heal Relationships
(George Faller and Heather P. Wright)

Waiting for Good News: Living with Chronic and Serious Illness
(Sally L. Wilke)

Preface

WELCOME TO a book about an experience that's very hard to welcome, job loss. Millions of people become unemployed every year, yet when job loss happens to us, we typically feel completely alone. That sense of isolation happens in part because no one knows how to comfort us when we lose our job. Unlike other griefs, such as a death, when someone can say, "I'm sorry for your loss," joblessness leaves the ones around us awkwardly at a loss for words.

We also feel alone because we typically don't tell others that we lost our job. Unless someone is a close friend or family member, they probably don't know, at least initially, about the unwanted change in our life. Feelings such as shame and fear attend the job loss, and we don't easily share those emotions.

Even those who do know about our job loss may feel powerless to help us or reticent to enter our sphere of hurt. After all, job loss can happen to anyone. Companies start up and close up at an amazing rate. Economic shifts and modern trends can decimate whole industries. Witnessing someone losing their job security reminds others of the fragility of their own financial status.

Welcome to a book written for you when you feel alone due to job loss. I'm sorry for your loss. You're not alone, though. I've been through the experience myself more than once. If you're like me, you will never forget this time of feeling uncertain and lost. From here on, you may always approach each job with a thought in the back of your head that the job might end. I trust that you will also never forget the ways that you find a path through this rough patch. I have plumbed my memories, and relied on the knowledge and wisdom of many others to write this book, to show you some paths we found, especially through faith. Your path will be your own, but I hope the ideas and reflections here get you started.

I must admit that returning to some of the fears and confusion of job loss to write this book felt hard. Two things kept me going. The first was you, the reader. I am a chaplain in my day job, so I know about listening to and walking with people through devastating losses. As I wrote these words, I not only remembered my own experience of job loss but also tried to recall others' and imagine yours. The best way to break the debilitating grip of job loss is to connect with other people. I trust that you are doing so in picking up this book. Believe it or not, many, many people care and can help get us back on our feet.

A second motivation kept me writing this book, even when I was at a loss for words of explanation and comfort about job loss. I realized that this was not my book, even if my name appears on the inside cover. This was God's book. When my words ended, God's words began. Prayers, insights, Bible stories, reflections, and intuition all arrived through the Holy Spirit so that I could share them with you. The experience amazed me, as being a vessel for God's work always does.

Welcome to a book about God's work, not just our own. In addition to a hunger for finding a job, we feel deeper longings to find purpose, to hear God's call. We yearn to be hired by God to deliver God's hope and peace to our world. Our yearning can be the glimmer of light buried in the darkness of job loss. Being forced to change our lives can spur our own growth and point us in a new employment direction that feels more authentic to who we are, can provide us with new skills of resilience, and can support us with a revived dependence on God.

Welcome to a book that wants you to not feel alone, that proclaims God's work, and that hopefully overlaps with your story. The first time I lost a job, I was a teacher who was last-hired-first-fired during the automobile-production downturn in Michigan. Amid empty summer days of missing my students and worrying about

The best way to break the debilitating grip of job loss is to connect with other people.

when I would teach again, I distracted myself by listening to a show on the radio called *A Radio Reader*. The show's host, Dick Estell, read books on the air for fifty-two years. He read books so beautifully that he could have been reading the phone book and we faithful listeners would still have tuned in. Each day I listened as Estell read the next passage of a thriller. As I awaited the climax of the story, I received word of a job interview. On the final day of that radio book reading, while Estell revealed the answer to the mystery, I interviewed for a new teaching job. After my interview I rushed to a bookstore (this was in the days before podcasts) and found the book so I could read the ending. Then I returned home to find a call on my answering machine. The teaching job was mine.

Our employment stories always overlap, as did the beginning of my new-job story with the end Dick Estell's story on the radio. That makes it all the better to tell our stories to the next person facing what we have faced and to share our best ideas for getting a new job. May the ideas and strategies in this book serve your needs, and may this book's story coincide with the beginning of new hope for yours.

Acknowledgments

With sincere gratitude . . .

- To God, who inspires my writing work.
- To Beth Gaede, whose editorial work and deep faith shape books and authors.
- To fellow chaplains and pastors, who have taught me so much at work.
- To parishioners, family, and friends, who shared their work journeys with me.
- To my spiritual director, Terri, who worked with me even when there was no work.
- And to my family—Chris, Molly, and June—who lived this book's story and who make all my work worthwhile.

Introduction

I REMEMBER every part of that fateful day. I was playing with our daughters in the living room when my husband came through the front door. I looked up, surprised to see him in the middle of the day. He didn't beat around the bush but quickly delivered the bad news, "I lost my job today." At that moment, the bottom dropped out of my world. We had two kids and a new mortgage. My husband had worked in the tech industry for many years, and we were spoiled by the computer boom in Seattle. But the recession had recently arrived and jobs were disappearing regularly. Now it was our turn to face job loss.

Over our many years of marriage, we had learned that we have classically divergent responses to crises. My husband underreacts, and I overreact. By that I mean he retreats into silence, and I go into a panicked tirade. Each of us tries to draw the other into our own style of response, but we are both hardwired to react in our set ways. This time was no different. I immediately wanted details, reasons, and answers for the job loss. What happened? What could we do? Would we be okay? My husband had no answers to my frightened questions. Looking back, I can feel compassion for the fact that he must have been hurting badly. But in that moment, all I could focus on was my own shock and despair.

In the computer-technology industry and many other organizations, once you lose your job, you are quickly shown to the door. Companies don't want you to have any time to leave with too much information. Therefore, there's no time for goodbyes or even desk-cleaning. Being ushered out the door without a minute to speak to longtime colleagues feels especially unfair.

When my husband arrived home that fateful day, he was already done working. No two-week notice or layoff notice. No escaping or slowly adjusting for either of us. After spewing questions for a while, I went for a walk or maybe a drive. I honestly don't remember which, so I hope it was a walk. I do remember that my predominant feeling was terror. What would we do? How would we maintain our lifestyle and pay for all the necessities and fun stuff? I knew my husband to be excellent at his job, being a math guy and all. But his job-finding skills were definitely subpar. I worked part-time and had committed to being with our young daughters as much as possible. So much to fear and to lose. I could barely breathe, so terrified was I about providing for our girls and sacrificing our livelihood.

Most of us who call ourselves "people of faith" want to believe that faith will be the answer during every hardship. However, losing a job and the economic security that goes with employment quickly demonstrates the fragility of our faith connection. My dependence on God's abundance seemed a very distant second to my reliance on the comfort and security of a regular paycheck, safe pension plan, and predictable life. Suddenly life thrust us into the unknown, and this proved a very shaky place to be. I looked around enviously at others who weren't walking this precarious path. Why couldn't I relax in the same blissful ignorance and sense of security they felt? Christ was supposed to be my sure foundation. I sang it in church and preached those words as a pastor. But faced with job loss, those words felt hollow and not at all capable of saving us from economic ruin.

How do we learn to trust God? We learn to trust God by recognizing that we learn to trust when we must and remembering that faith practices "work," whether or not we can work. Determined to worship the God of the Bible, rather than the god of Wall Street, I threw myself into prayer. I uttered desperate prayers for calm during my initial walks. "Please, please, please make this right," I begged God.

We also prayed with our kids. This was so very important to me—to show them that on the day Dad lost his job, we prayed. I wanted our

> We learn to trust God by recognizing that we learn to trust when we must and remembering that faith practices "work," whether or not we can work.

girls to have this model of prayer from their childhood to remember later when they grew up and faced their own crises. I trusted that prayer would give us enough stopgap peace to get us to the next step. God delivered on my trust. Now I share the story and lessons with you.

Our family's experience of job loss, and a larger societal picture of job loss, reveals several key issues that we will explore in this book:

- Job loss forces us to feel a wide range of emotions.
- Job loss invites us to understand the nature of work.
- Job loss leads us to find spiritual resources.
- Job loss challenges us to carve out a path from joblessness to employment.

Job Loss Forces Us into a Wide Range of Emotions

Under stress, we regress.

Hospital chaplains witness a basic phenomenon every day as patients and families face various crises. The phenomenon can be summarized in four words: "Under stress, we regress." The same truth can apply to people experiencing crises beyond the hospital setting, such as job loss. Unfortunately, the majority of people who find themselves suddenly jobless don't have a chaplain to help them with all the regressing that stress like job loss triggers (although some large companies do, in fact, hire chaplains for their employees). Therefore, people who lose their jobs often suffer alone at home, reverting to unhealthy, reactive modes.

When "under stress we regress," our loved ones also pay the price for whatever type of regression we tend toward. As I mentioned earlier, when faced with the shock and stress of job loss, my husband and I definitely regressed into our old patterns, ingrained during many years of marriage. My husband, as expected, snapped into shutdown mode. I knew he was hiding deep inside himself somewhere, nursing his wounds. But I had no idea how to reach him. And besides, I wasn't even focused on comforting him. I felt too busy seeking relief from the overwrought feelings and fears inside of me and looking for someone to blame.

In a perfect world, someone who seems uber calm like my husband would naturally balance someone like me, who responds immediately and dramatically to hard news. But the last time I checked, this was certainly not a perfect world. Spouses/partners know that better than most. So rather than balancing or helping each other, we got stuck in our own ways of facing problems. Fortunately, we could later look back and notice how we gradually moved from taking job loss out on each other to trying to support each other.

When each of us acknowledges that "under stress we each regress … differently," some critical wisdom and forgiveness can surface. Our different reactions can ultimately lead to a larger palette of skills that are essential to working one's way through crises such as unemployment.

We need all the skills we can muster, because when we lose our jobs a multitude of feelings come rushing in and engulf us! For example, there's the powerful sense of grief that seems to completely knock us over when we first lose our job. As much as we complain about the grind of daily work, when our work routines are yanked away from us, we feel quite disoriented. There's no "there" there, the place to go to work—in our cars and on our subways and even down the hall to the spare bedroom. No purposeful place to stimulate our minds and help us delineate work from the rest of our lives.

One of the first griefs in job loss, therefore, feels very physical. Our bodies can no longer rely on the movement of commuting from home place to work place. As a result, our minds get confused and ask, "Why don't I have anywhere I have to go?" Minds that are stressed from the job loss become even more rattled when there's not a physical outlet to help ease the worries and to-do's.

Depending on how we felt about our work, we might also experience a major loss of purpose. Perhaps we were teachers or social workers whose work involved a daily commitment to improving others' lives. We miss both our students and the joy of seeing the light go on in their eyes when they master new skills.

As much as we complain about the grind of daily work, when our work routines are yanked away from us, we feel quite disoriented.

One of the first griefs in job loss, therefore, feels very physical.

When our stream of purpose and community suddenly begins to dry up, our identity seems to become shallower and less predictable.

It's no wonder we feel lost amidst job loss. We can't begin to see the future, and we must endure the pain of the unknown in the present.

When our stream of purpose and community suddenly begins to dry up, our identity seems to become shallower and less predictable. We may do our best to control that process, futilely attempting to counteract whatever circumstances stole our work and stopped us in our progress, frantically trying to gather up our dissipating self-respect and confidence.

Meanwhile, our feelings about job loss multiply even further. We miss our colleagues from work and feel so many emotions toward them, including envy, estrangement, and shame. We miss silly little things that we had no idea were giving our lives daily meaning and structure. The friendly bus driver. Our penchant for unsticking the copy machine. Asking our coworkers about their weekend. Unemployment represents a giant, scary question mark with no sentence written following it.

It's no wonder we feel lost amidst job loss. We can't begin to see the future, and we must endure the pain of the unknown in the present. Never mind whether we felt fulfilled in our work or always got along with our coworkers. Never mind that we thought numerous times about finding work with more depth, fewer miles on the road, better childcare. The choice to leave should have been our decision to make, not our boss's or the administration's. The doubts and blame eat at us.

Just reading about all these job-loss-related feelings might possibly plunge us deeper into despair. Just so you know, that's definitely not our purpose here! Which is why this book is called *Jobs Lost, Faith Found*. This book provides a reminder that we can rely on the good news poured out through our holy text and spiritual leaders. As followers of the One always willing to listen and guide us, we receive lifesaving portions of God's grace. God delivers this grace through many means, including Bible stories and prayers. We explore those Bible stories in this book, and garner the lessons found there to help us abide and learn from our feelings.

- What feelings have you experienced during job loss?
- What did you do with those feelings?
- How do your responses to stress differ from your spouse's or friends'?
- How does it help to know that others are going through similar feelings?
- What Bible stories and spiritual readings help you name and understand your feelings?

In chapter 1, "Dealing with Our Feelings about Job Loss," we will expand on these ideas and questions.

Job Loss Invites Us to Understand the Nature of Work

When we lose a job, we lose so much more than a job. That's because work is so essential to our being. Work shapes our lives with purpose, structure, creativity, teamwork, the common good, legacy, beginnings–middles–ends, labor, sacrifice, and God-given gifts. No wonder losing work cuts us to the quick. St. Benedict, the fifth-century patron saint of Europe, wrote guidelines for monks called the Rule of St. Benedict. The role of work occupied a central place in Benedict's guidelines, as demonstrated in his words, "To work is to pray; to pray is to work." Our humanity, our faith, and our work entwine so tightly that when we look at one strand in this three-part configuration, we find the other strands as well.

Work includes countless aspects essential to our very being. Therefore, we can look at work from one angle after another. For example, as I relive the story of our family's job loss, I'm struck by the way that the theme of time runs through the experience. When my husband lost his job, I instantly worried about the long-term effects of the change, having just signed a thirty-year mortgage. Meanwhile, my husband had no time to achieve a sense of closure or say goodbye to his colleagues. Time got turned upside down on layoff day. The beating metronome of steady lives slid off the piano and crashed onto the floor. This phenomenon of "ordinary" time being upended occurs in many crises. That's why we need to find a new normal that can stabilize and return some sense of regular time and rhythm to our lives.

> When we lose a job, we lose so much more than a job.

> Our humanity, our faith, and our work entwine so tightly that when we look at one strand in this three-part configuration, we find the other strands as well.

In job loss, the sting of time turned upside down can be particularly unnerving. Deadlines remain for bills to be paid and kids to be fed, yet we can't make employers offer us jobs any more quickly. Meanwhile we are struggling to re-create the structure for our time that work provided. We may never have realized how jobs ordered our lives, even though we complained about our work as "the grind."

To work is to pray; to pray is to work. St. Benedict reminded us that as spiritual beings, we find work as basic a human need as communicating with God. Our work is interconnected with our sense of being alive, connected, and useful, so we can reflect on work through a spiritual lens. Here's an example of God's followers doing just that. At the Center for Work and Faith in New York City, people of faith explore the roots of work as an embodiment of faith:

> Faith and work. We might them see as estranged. But, in truth, they share a crucial aim: to see the unseen. Nothing new has been made without faith. Nothing unseen has been seen without work. When the force of what we do hits why we do it, we wither or we flourish. We don't want to just examine that collision. We want to live in the intersection where it occurs. To celebrate what flies. And to rethink what falls. To map. To explore. To create. To risk and to fail better. Not just for a nicer 9-to-5. But to serve the city we belong to and love. It comes down to one key truth: work matters. So do it well. (https://faithandwork.com)

From a spiritual perspective, work occupies a powerful place in our lives that goes way beyond paying the bills. As Christians, we don't just say we hold down a job; we say we fulfill a vocation. We dare to believe that God calls us to our work and service, and empowers us to make a difference for others no matter what our jobs. Given that undergirding faith, the gut-punch of job loss can be especially confusing and disappointing from a faith perspective. We come up with newly relevant questions for God about how to complete our calling when employment slams the door on our God-given dreams.

We need to find a new normal that can stabilize and return some sense of regular time and rhythm to our lives.

- What has job loss taught you about what work means to you?
- How does St. Benedict's Rule, "To work is to pray; to pray is to work?," resonate with your work?
- In what ways has time felt different when you are not working?
- Who do you know who talks about a job as a call?

In chapter 2, "Thinking about Why We Work," we will expand on these ideas and questions.

Finding our way back to work not only relieves financial fears; it aligns us with God's creativity and sense of purpose.

Job Loss Leads Us to Find Spiritual Resources

We named this book *Jobs Lost, Faith Found* because during encounters with joblessness (as well as a number of other challenges), we discover a wealth of spiritual resources within and beyond ourselves. In other words, the nature of joblessness shows us:

- What we are made of
- What God is made of

When we endure unemployment and are pared down to our innermost selves, our lives become quickly devoid of the trappings that we assumed were saving us. In this raw moment, we can consciously or unconsciously take stock of what remains. As surely as anything, this moment calls upon the faith we have been given— and hopefully have nurtured. Marc Kolden (1930–2017), longtime professor of systematic theology at Luther Seminary, Saint Paul, Minnesota, often offered this definition of "faith" in his lectures and personal conversations with students and others: not knowing what will happen and how we will come through can be just the moment we reinforce what we do know—that we are lost without a relationship with God, a relationship characterized by trust, openness, and joy—that allows us to face the future with peace.

When life reduces itself to its very core during a crisis such as job loss, we find out what God is made of. God is made of comfort. God offers us solace to focus on what we have, rather than what

As Christians, we don't just say we hold down a job; we say we fulfill a vocation. We dare to believe that God calls us to our work and service, and empowers us to make a difference for others no matter what our jobs.

we don't have. In gratitude we notice the smallest things. "Thank you, God," we pray, "for the food in the freezer, the neighbors who greet us as they normally do, our families whom we can count on, the soft pillow where we can rest our head and forget our cares for a few hours. Thank you for your blessings that have always sustained us, even when we assumed it was all up to us and our employment."

What we are made of also becomes starkly evident as we regroup via rituals and relationships during our search for employment. And as we realize our own vulnerability and grit, we also get additional glimpses of what God is made of. Perhaps God's language of silence seems deafening as we overnight-deliver our prayers for survival and quick fixes. But somehow God leads us to put one foot in front of another. Life shocked us, yet we are still standing and the universe keeps spinning. Creativity and surprises arrive. Small parcels of blessings arrive at our door. God attends to us, and maybe wonders whether we will interpret the mysteries as divine provision. Whether we will witness to another about the balm in Gilead. This is the time to learn just how durable, ingenious, and other-than-us is this God of whom we have spoken and whom we now get to know.

My husband's and my prayers seemed like all we had to share with our children in the time of job loss. We never guessed that we were sharing more riches with them in that moment than we had when that regular paycheck was arriving every two weeks. If we had not gone through that hard time, when would we have felt compelled to demonstrate to our daughters that God is the bedrock of our lives? All the learning they completed in Sunday school and all the worship services they attended surely shaped our daughters' lives. But in a moment of crisis, our faith lessons became especially real. Our hopes for our children's faith and endurance were exactly what bolstered our faith and endurance.

Job loss is a particular crisis flavor, but sooner or later most of us taste the truth that life includes events we never would have chosen. When crises such as job loss are thrust upon us unexpectedly, we can turn to God through various spiritual practices, practices named

> God offers us solace to focus on what we have, rather than what we don't have.

"an alphabet of spiritual tools" in this book. Through these spiritual practices, God invites us to be creative and think differently. God wants to "keep the faith" for each of us. So God enlightens us by showing us that what we *don't have* is exactly what we *do* have. What we don't have is a job. This certainly feels like terrible news. But wait! What we do have is a situation that forces and invites us to partner with God and craft creative solutions. The necessity of learning and providing propels us into territory and faith we may not have sought while we lived in our comfort zone. Creativity is born of limits and tight places, like joblessness. Undoubtedly you have developed your own cadre of creative solutions over the course of your life.

The writers of a late-night talk show faced a daily deadline of coming up with a stand-up comedy routine for the show's host. An interviewer asked the writers if they sat around all day telling jokes. The writers replied that thankfully they only had an hour each morning to write. That short preparation time provided exactly the limit they needed to focus on creativity.

Joblessness offers similar built-in limits—on our time, money, and control—that can inspire creativity. Looking at limits as gifts rather than deficits is actually a spiritual way to live. That's because God always invites us to see things differently and offers to show us a new picture through limits of living in obedience, justice, and truth.

Job Loss Challenges Us to Carve Out a Path from Joblessness to Employment

In addition to its initial chapters on the feelings of job loss, the meaning of work, and the spiritual tools that help us grow from job loss, this book includes a chapter on navigating the process of finding new work. We call this chapter "Ten Questions to Help You Get from Here (No Job) to There (Job)."

Given the decades that we participate in the work world, it makes sense that most of us face periods of economic change and even

This is the time to learn just how durable, ingenious, and other-than-us is this God of whom we have spoken and whom we now get to know.

Creativity is born of limits and tight places, like joblessness.

Even though we feel shocked and alone when we become the victims of financial sea change, we are not actually alone.

job loss. The truth is that markets rise and fall, and economies wax and wane. Even though we feel shocked and alone when we become the victims of financial sea change, we are not actually alone. We share the good company of others over the centuries who have endured this hard process. This can be comforting to remember from the start of our joblessness. Because we humans in general are natural controllers, our feelings and questions rush in immediately: What did I do? How did I fail? Recognizing that the systems beyond our control can affect us gives us a bit of necessary perspective from the start.

Joblessness can feel like driving along and encountering a major traffic jam. Suddenly we join a line of barely moving cars and have no idea what happened up ahead. Eventually we again begin to inch along, although not very patiently or hopefully. Our endurance skills somehow sustain us until we realize that the situation is righting itself, albeit slowly. We console ourselves by remembering that if there weren't *some* movement up ahead, we would be even farther back. Miles back. So we wait, and trust, and try not to get too frustrated during the process until finally we're cruising (and working) again.

From the beginning of our encounter with job loss, our family's story mirrored countless others' situations. Plenty of families felt the sting of a high-tech bust. And while our experiences were painful, our stories undoubtedly paled in comparison to the stories of those whose unemployment was chronic, or who lived in families where multiple generations of people were unemployed or underemployed. With newfound compassion, we suddenly realized connections between ourselves and others that we never wanted to think about before. For instance, we too worried about making ends meet at the grocery store and considered asking for a scholarship for a school field trip. Losing a job also left us to wonder, What must life be like when the uncertainty goes on and on? How painful is the poverty of purpose for young people struggling to find hope? One of the greatest legacies of job loss can be staying motivated to advocate for others to find well-paid, purposeful employment.

The question of how tight the social safety net is becomes a much more personal topic during job loss, as does the viability of family support systems. We suddenly find out what services our cities may offer and whether we have cultivated the kinds of friendships and communities that endure when the going gets rough.

When we face a crisis such as unemployment, these support systems become evident and essential. We quickly realize who's available, from babysitters to those willing to lend an ear. Just like in many other arenas of our lives, we don't know what we need until we need it. Our support systems can be rusty or nonexistent. Cultivating relationships when we are feeling vulnerable ourselves can be hard, but that's often exactly how life happens. Our humility can open the door to others' understanding and willingness to help.

Faith communities, ideally, can provide natural support systems. That's because people of faith are taught to love our neighbors and live out Christ's mission in tangible acts of service. Faith communities can be places where spiritual leaders know how to tap volunteer skills and organize teams. Undoubtedly someone at church would be more than willing to drive us to the work counselor when we don't have transportation. We just need to connect with that volunteer. It's probably someone we see in the pews on Sunday morning.

Churches can also provide natural places where those suffering joblessness can go to find a listening ear and support groups. Faith leaders are trained to listen to the story of our short-term and long-

Our humility can open the door to others' understanding and willingness to help.

term employment journeys and to help us figure out the next steps. Others who have faced, or who currently face, similar situations can become valuable resources, for they respond with actual experience and without judgment.

During the weeks of joblessness when we are sorting out our feelings, tapping our resources, and growing in faith, we are also forming a vision of how to get from unemployment back to employment. The vision includes simply getting through each day and making ends meet, as well as adopting a broader perspective than we had before the crisis. Naming new goals and figuring out the steps to achieve them is part of the process. Finding out that we have visions and can realize them is one of the true epiphanies in the midst of loss and change.

Finding out that we have visions and can realize them is one of the true epiphanies in the midst of loss and change.

But how do we translate visions into action plans? There's a process to follow and this book names the process! Get organized, write a resumé, search job sites, discover your network of friends and neighbors, craft cover letters, prepare for interviews, meet with potential employers, thank everyone who helps you, and learn to wait. Several sources could help you figure out how to do these things. In this book we've added a spiritual dimension, such as praying for others and collaborating with church support groups.

When my husband lost his job, our family learned firsthand how job loss can hit hard and knock us over. This book begins with that reality and offers ways to deal with joblessness. Specifically, these ways include attending to our feelings and relationships, understanding the broader meaning of work, relying on spiritual strategies, and learning how to take the necessary steps to find get back in the workforce. By offering these reflections and ideas, we want to provide you with hope. This book is part of a series of books called Living with Hope. By using what we've discerned through hard times to help others, each of us is called to pass on hope. That's part of our spiritual work, whether or not we have a "day job."

- Why are churches well equipped to help members dealing with job loss?
- What concrete help do you need to navigate the job search process?
- When have you taken advantage of a support group to help you through a tough time?
- Who could you turn to in your faith community to just talk?

In chapter 4, "Ten Questions to Help You Get from Here (No Job) to There (Job)," we will expand on these ideas and questions.

May the ideas you find here combine with your God-given wisdom and knowledge to lead you to live out the work to which God calls you.

Resources

The Center for Faith and Work, New York City. faithandwork.com.

- Explores the intersection of our employment and our belief systems through workshops, newsletters, and conferences.

The Rule of St. Benedict. https://tinyurl.com/msndn49.

- Written in the sixth century, this continues to serve as a guideline for monastic Christians in the Order of St. Benedict.

1

Dealing with Our Feelings about Job Loss

WHEN WE go through the trauma of job loss and the slog of a job search, we all experience a wide variety of feelings. We may wonder if others are going through all this emotional turbulence, and the truth is that everyone who faces this tough situation gets on a roller coaster of ups and downs. In this chapter we will take a look at several of the feelings that people go through during unemployment and reemployment. Each of us is different, but as humans we share many core emotions. During situations of loss, these feelings can seem especially acute.

Finding someone with whom to share our pain and challenges when so many feelings pile up inside us can be really helpful. A professional counselor or a support group can assist us, and certainly trusted friends and close family members can help us through the rough patches. Companies sometimes refer laid-off employees to job transition specialists who can help us make a plan and gather further resources. Life coaches who focus on job loss also bring valuable experience and a familiarity with key issues.

In addition to finding people who can walk with us through joblessness, we can also express some of our feelings by journaling about what's going on each day. Writing about our honest emotions helps us sort the feelings out and enables us to turn them into prayers. Journaling can also help us gain some perspective on our feelings, so they feel more manageable.

Perhaps you've always wanted to start a journaling process, or have let your writing practice lapse. Now is the perfect time to begin again. We can choose to pay more for a fancy journal or simply pick up a cheap notebook. To get our writing hand moving, we can set a timer for ten minutes (or even less). Journalers can produce a surprising number of words and ideas in ten minutes.

Writing prompts offer us an opening line from which to start. We can use the following prompts during our journaling time, or come up with our own:

- If I could have any job . . .
- I am most worried about . . .
- What others think I need is . . . , but what I really need is . . .
- If I could tell my old bosses exactly what I think . . .
- The things I miss most about my old workplace are . . .
- If I could ask God anything, I would ask . . .
- The things I don't miss about my old workplace are . . .
- I feel relieved that . . .
- If my kids face this experience of job loss someday . . .

Journaling can also help us gain some perspective on our feelings, so they feel more manageable.

We can also use "fast writes" as a fun way to get our minds percolating. In this case, the timer is set for two minutes and we write as quickly as our minds and hands can move, using one word as a theme. For instance, we could write for two minutes about any of these words: *job*, *dream*, *hope*, *secret*, and *share*. The time limit of two minutes forces us to think fast, which can inspire creativity. Remember, our journaling is not meant to be award-winning writing. The practice is meant to give our souls the space and time to express deep feelings.

Whenever we write, and for however long we write, the practice of writing can unearth some of the feelings we are holding inside. The experience enables us to begin to name the challenges and opportunities we face.

So what are some of the common feelings that we experience in job loss and job searches? We will explore eight feelings: fear, shame, relief, confusion, resistance, vulnerability, hopelessness, and gratitude. As we focus on each feeling, we will consider some biblical texts and spiritual readings, include psalm verses and prayers, and offer helpful questions for journaling.

Fear

The sleeping giant of fear is instantly awakened when we face unemployment. After all, we are brushing up against a primal need for survival. Of course we are afraid. It would be truly startling if we were not afraid. The question is not whether we feel fear, but how to manage our fear. Two biblical models can help us learn to manage our fears.

The first model is David in the story of his encounter with Goliath (1 Samuel 17). This familiar tale begins with King Saul and his army facing off against their enemy, the Philistines. The Philistine troops include a gigantic man named Goliath. No one on King Saul's side dares to fight Goliath, until David, a young shepherd, volunteers for the job. In spite of everyone's doubts, David relies on his keen aim with a slingshot and slays Goliath with a smooth stone launched at Goliath's forehead.

When we stare up at the behemoth called unemployment, we undoubtedly feel as minuscule as David facing the giant. So how did David prevail? The story suggests it was his skill with the slingshot and his keen aim. That's what most of us remember. But scratch the surface of this tale and discover the deeper reason that David could face up to his fear. David remembered how he protected his sheep from harm because God empowered him to do so.

When we study the story further, one of the fascinating details is that David refused to wear a suit of armor provided by Saul when he went out to face Goliath. Why? Because the armor was too big for him. David could only deal with his fear in ways that fit who David was. During joblessness, we may receive lots of advice or even offers of help that don't seem to "fit" our situation. Like David, we

Remember, our journaling is not meant to be award-winning writing. The practice is meant to give our souls the space and time to express deep feelings.

need to be aware that another's sense of protection may be different from our own. Ultimately, God invites us to trust the "armor" that God provides for each of us.

Ephesians 6 tells us to "put on the whole armor of God." In my work as a chaplain, I've realized that the armor of God can be a hospital gown, of all things. Wait! How can such a flimsy garment qualify as the armor of God? Hospital gowns reveal God's protection in three ways:

1. Hospital gowns are great equalizers. Rich or poor, old or young—we all look the same in a hospital gown. God protects us by reminding us of our common identity as children of God.
2. Hospital gowns provide a very thin covering. God protects us by showing us our dependence on others, rather than putting thick barriers between others and us.
3. Hospital gowns give us no place to hide. God protects us by reminding us of our humanity and dependence on God.

> During joblessness, we may receive lots of advice or even offers of help that don't seem to fit our situation.

During many days of joblessness, we can feel as vulnerable as a patient in a hospital gown. That's the time to remember that God's idea of armor can be nontraditional and can actually "fit" our needs.

The second biblical model for managing fear is Mary, the mother of Jesus. We read in Luke 2 about the angel Gabriel visiting Mary to let her know that she has been chosen to give birth to God's Son, Immanuel. Immediately, the perceptive angel tells Mary not to be afraid. Come again?! Any of us would be astounded, perplexed, and shaken to the core by this news that our world (and *the* world) was about to change. As we continue the story, we find out what Mary does with her feelings of awe and uncertainty. She travels to visit her cousin Elizabeth, who is also expecting a baby. Mary doesn't stay home and stoke her fears; she goes to find community where she can express her faith and doubts.

When Mary arrives at her cousin's home, she moves from fear to proclamation. Yes, it will be daunting to give birth to God's son! But

Mary shares her movement from fear to faith in the words of the Magnificat:

> My soul magnifies the Lord,
> And my spirit rejoices in God my Savior,
> For he has looked with favor on the lowliness of his servant.
> Surely, from now on all generations will call me blessed;
> For the Mighty One has done great things for me,
>   and holy is his name.
> His mercy is for those who fear him from generation to generation.
> (Luke 1:46–50)

Mary witnessed to God's work in her life and the coming of Emmanuel. The drastic change in her life could be used for God's glory.

Both David, the young shepherd, and Mary, the mother of Jesus, found assistance for their fears through memories of God's help in the past and a vision of God's work in the future. We can ponder their stories as we reach out to God with our fears, recall the way that God has protected us in the past, and imagine the good news that God can deliver in our future.

> I sought the Lord, and he answered me,
>   and delivered me from all my fears.
> (Ps 34:4)

Both David, the young shepherd, and Mary, the mother of Jesus, found assistance for their fears through memories of God's help in the past and a vision of God's work in the future.

Prayer

Let nothing disturb you,
Let nothing frighten you,
All things are passing away:
God never changes.
Patience obtains all things
Whoever has God lacks nothing;
God alone suffices.
—St. Teresa of Ávila[1]

Questions for Journaling

What am I afraid of?

What has helped me deal with my fears in the past?

With whom have I shared my fears?

Where can I go to find a calm place?

Shame

Losing employment or not being able to find a job can definitely make us feel "less than." We tend to blame ourselves for whatever happened and can find it difficult to share our travails because of our injured pride. Shame then stymies us from moving forward. This happened for Harry. He worked as an advertising executive in a Chicago ad agency. During his thirty years with the company, he dressed up in a suit and rode the train to his downtown office every day from the northern suburbs. After Harry was laid off, he felt so mortified that he continued his routine—dressing in a suit and riding the train downtown. He didn't even tell his family about his dismissal until he had no choice but to share the bad news.

We may also turn our shame outward and feel intense envy of others whose lives appear more secure at the moment. This feels especially troubling because we don't want to seem bitter or humorless. Therefore, we may find ourselves drawing away from old friends and coworkers, assuming that they won't be able to understand our situation.

When we examine our shame more closely, we come face to face with our old assumption that we were in control or had all the resources and answers we would ever need. When those illusions are shattered, we feel like we've let ourselves down, not to mention the family members who depend on us.

God takes no pleasure in our shame but welcomes our shame as a road into the truth that we were never saving ourselves in the first place. We once lived with the naive belief that we were caring for ourselves because we earned a paycheck.

In fact, all of our provisions, including our health, food, homes, and paychecks, begin with God's abundance. Really? That's hard to sort out! We are supposed to work very hard, and we understandably feel very proud when our efforts are rewarded. So we naturally attribute our blessings to our own grit, rather than to God's generosity.

However, our temporary successes aren't the same as God's unconditional love. While we may feel justified by our efforts and pride ourselves on our successes, God doesn't measure us in this way. God loves us whether or not we have a job, a plan, a resumé, or a 401(k). God loved us before our last job and will love us after our next job. Our love for ourselves, and pride in ourselves, understandably wavers with our circumstances. But God's love for us is solid. We can lose our job, but we can't lose God's love.

The story of the woman at the well (John 4) reminds us of Jesus's nonjudgmental attitude. In this story, Jesus encounters a Samaritan woman at a well on a very hot day. He asks her for a drink of water, which surprises the woman because Jesus is Jewish. Jews and Samaritans saw each other as adversaries in Jesus's time. Yet she hands Jesus a cup of water, and they enter a spiritual conversation. Jesus promises to give the woman another kind of water that he calls "living water." She is intrigued and finds Jesus's words full of promise. He surprises the woman even further when he tells her about her own life, including the fact that she has had several husbands. The woman at the well (we never know her name) finds Jesus's knowledge and acceptance miraculous. Her life is deemed shameful by the world's standards, yet Jesus offers her living water. And she accepts his offer. She is thirsty for grace. We are similarly thirsty for grace when we isolate ourselves, bound by guilt, helplessness, and the false belief that we are self-sufficient. When the woman at the well drinks of Jesus's message of unconditional acceptance and love, she is so moved that she goes to tell others about Jesus.

God takes no pleasure in our shame but welcomes our shame as a road into the truth that we were never saving ourselves in the first place.

Deep inside our shame, we often become confused. We think we did something wrong (sinned) and that's why we lost our jobs. In truth, that's not likely the case. God forgives us our sins and intends that we should let go of our shame. When we confess the ways we have truly failed ourselves and others (sin), we can more easily let go of imagined failures (shame) that lock us into a dead end. The psalmists, and the liturgists, wrote prayers of confession. Their words offer an exit strategy from our vicious cycle of being ashamed of our shame. When we confess our sins at church, or in a private rite, we surrender to God both our real and perceived failures. Then we hear God's blessed news proclaimed by a spiritual leader: we are forgiven. That news washes over us like living water, cleansing us from the reality of sin and the secret of shame.

> Create in me a clean heart, O God, and renew in me a right spirit.
> (Ps 51:10)

Prayer

Dear God,
Today somebody is suffering, today somebody is in the street, today somebody is hungry.
Our work is for today, yesterday has gone, tomorrow has not yet come—*today*, we have only *today* to make Jesus known, loved, served, fed, clothed, and sheltered. Amen
—Mother Teresa[3]

Questions for Journaling

What am I ashamed of?

Have I given my shame to God?

How is it hurting me to keep envying others?

Who has taught me about God's unconditional love? What have I learned?

Relief

The experience of job loss and job searching can obviously be heartbreaking, terrifying, and confounding. Yet there's another possibility. Sometimes job loss can actually be a liberating relief. Maybe we've felt locked into an unfulfilling job by "golden handcuffs" or our resistance to change. Perhaps God has been nudging us for a while to make a move, and job loss has finally brought that inkling to fruition. Sometimes we watch other people become the victims of downsizing and become more and more anxious (and less and less productive) waiting for our turn. When the inevitable layoff finally happens, we feel a sense of relief about no longer facing the unknown.

For whatever reason, relief can become part of the picture in job loss, which can of course trigger other feelings, like guilt about our sense of relief. Where do we put relief within the range of feelings about job loss? Relief can certainly tip the scales in a slightly more positive direction than other feelings we have named, like despair and powerlessness. Unlike these more debilitating sensations, relief carries an inherent energy that urges us to move forward from whatever job or experience was not giving us relief. Seeking a more stimulating and satisfying work experience can spark our creativity and trigger a healthy discernment process. Relief sounds like a relief, doesn't it? Especially in comparison to paralyzing fear or stubborn resistance!

Sometimes the relief of job loss arrives in a totally unexpected way. This was the case for Renée, who puzzled long and hard over whether to sacrifice her old, secure job when she was offered a new job. Renée prayed and talked to friends as she attempted to discern her next move. Finally she experienced a wave of bravery and resigned from her old job. The relief of being willing to take a risk buoyed her during the following months, when she sold her house and moved to another state to start her new position.

The first weeks at the company proved rocky, and it quickly dawned on Renée that she had stepped into a dysfunctional organization. She hung in there, hoping that the conflicts would settle down and she would feel good about her move. When the circumstances did not improve, Renée prayed a new prayer: "God, please give me the courage to stay or the courage to go." After more weeks and months of trying, Renée finally resigned her position. Rather than feeling panicked, she experienced another palpable sense of relief that God had provided her the strength to say no to something that would never work out. Although Renée's path seemed to twist and turn, rather than follow a straight trajectory, she felt relieved to have taken a chance and launched herself out of security and into an active dependence on her faith.

What are other faith stories that teach us about relief from a spiritual perspective? Many stories of saints can inform us. For example, Martin Luther's vocational path included chapters of relief. Luther's father wanted him to study law, but Luther felt called to be a monk. In the end, Luther found relief when he dropped out of

> Sometimes job loss can actually be a liberating relief.

Martin Luther's vocational path included chapters of relief.

law school to study philosophy and theology. Luther also struggled with his own inner demons of never being good enough or working hard enough. Indeed, God delivered relief to Luther when he finally quit trying to earn God's approval (and his own approval) through never-ending labor. Luther's theology of grace was partially spurred by his own need for relief. He felt an enormous sense of gratitude when he discovered that God could lead him in a path of righteousness beyond Luther's own making. Luther's hymn lyrics point to his trust in the God of grace: "A mighty fortress is our God, / A bulwark never failing, / Our helper He amid the flood, / Of mortal ills prevailing."[4]

Most of us find a sliver of good news (relief) even in the midst of bad news like job loss. Being honest about our relief and discovering what we were happy to leave behind informs us about what we want and need in the future.

> He put a new song in my mouth, a song of praise to our God.
> (Ps 40:3)

Prayer

May today there be peace within.
May you trust God that you are exactly where you are meant to be.
May you not forget the infinite possibilities that are born of faith.
May you use those gifts that you have received, and pass on the love that has been given to you.
May you be content knowing you are a child of God.
Let this presence settle into your bones, and allow your soul the freedom to sing, dance, praise and love.
It is there for each and every one of us.
—Teresa of Ávila[5]

Questions for Journaling

What are some jobs I've always wanted to pursue?

How long have I been unsatisfied with my work? Why?

What natural gifts do I have that I haven't been using?

Who could serve as a mentor as I strike out in new paths?

Confusion

Where to begin the process of dealing with job loss and looking for a new job? That question can perplex even the most intrepid person when faced with the emptiness of unemployment. One must simultaneously provide stopgap measures for the present and image a new future. Sounds mindboggling—because it is. We are looking back, looking around, and looking ahead. No wonder it's so hard to focus!

Seems a bit counterintuitive in a book about unemployment to learn from the example of those who voluntarily left their work, but here goes. In the early chapters of the Gospels, such as Matthew 4, Luke 5, and John 1, we find stories of Jesus calling his first disciples. Jesus's powerful spirit and simple invitation, "come and see," compelled those first followers to drop their fishing nets and livelihoods and pursue a holy vocation. The path of discipleship that Jesus offered certainly did not prove to be easy or obvious. Instead, the followers experienced risk, mystery, and the very heart of life and death. But Jesus's disciples' confusion about what to do with their lives was counteracted by a commitment to follow in the path of love and a reliance on Jesus to lead them.

Days of job searches can be fraught with millions of questions. *How do I find job openings? Is anyone interested in my skills? Who can help me write a resumé?* But having some simple phrases to return to when your brain is overflowing can be just what you need. These phrases can both focus us for job seeking and keep us grounded in the faith and discipleship that enlivens us. For example, Psalm 16:11 states, "You show me the path of life." The path of life may be revealed a few inches at a time, so enormous patience and many restarts are required. Still, to have something to cling to during times of confusion can be absolutely life-giving.

> But Jesus's disciples' confusion about what to do with their lives was counteracted by a commitment to follow in the path of love and a reliance on Jesus to lead them.

The path of life may be revealed a few inches at a time, so enormous patience and many restarts are required.

We can explore the phrases we choose by writing about them in our journal or sharing them with our friends. We can also get out of the confusion in our heads by drawing simple diagrams. We can sketch our path as it stands and note some of the places we have been. As we go from being lost in our head to a little note found on a piece of paper or whiteboard, we find a new tool to deal with our confusion. God's word and our simple action can help us become more ingenious in navigating the newly complicated landscape.

The verse "You show me the path of life" took on a special meaning for me during a long bike trip a decade ago. I felt nervous about whether I could ride hundreds of miles, so I turned to the Psalms for help. I printed the words "You show me the path of life" on a piece of paper and displayed that message in the clear map compartment on top of my handlebar bag. By doing so, I could easily glance down and be encouraged by the psalm verse. There was just one problem. My handlebar bag didn't fit properly and kept slipping out of place. Finally, during a rest stop, I moved the bag from my handlebars and attached it to the back of my bike seat. A crazy thing began to happen! Other riders read the words of the psalm verse and mentioned them to me. Whether we know it or not, when we follow God's path of life, we become witnesses to the truth of letting God lead us. We discover how many other people are also looking for guidance to escape their confusion.

Another strategy for dealing with confusion involves relying on the wisdom of elders. Many towns and cities offer job seekers help from retired business people. For free! The retirees are eager to help others carve out their path of life, and provide solid skills in marketing, employment searches, and follow-up strategies. They can also practice the most important skill—listening. When we talk about our confusion and someone listens, we begin to articulate our own answers. We just needed someone (and ourselves) to hear the ideas.

You show me the path of life.
(Ps 16:11)

Prayer

O God, you have called your servants to ventures of which we cannot see the ending, by paths as yet untrodden, through perils unknown. Give us faith to go out with good courage, not knowing where we go, but only that your hand is leading us and your love supporting us; through Jesus Christ our Lord. Amen[6]

Questions for Journaling

Make a list of ten things you want to do to find a job.

Draw a lifeline of your work history and look for patterns there.

If someone came to you to tell you about losing their job, what advice would you give them?

What do you imagine that God desires for you?

Resistance

The magnitude of dealing with unemployment and seeking a job can make us want to pull a blanket over our head and just ignore the realities. Denial about our situation can inspire us to become stubbornly complacent. This is completely understandable, because the experience of losing a job can be so debilitating. Everyone deserves a little time to regroup under a cozy quilt. The problem comes when we burrow deeper and deeper onto the couch and can't seem to get up. It may seem like our muscles, and our life, are atrophying in that position. In truth, we are building a very conniving muscle—the muscle of resistance.

As we become better and better at resisting the actions needed to find a job—because we are sad, overwhelmed, alone, resentful—we get further and further in trouble. We fail to call on God, or anyone else. Sounds strange, but we simultaneously think we're not worth helping and also think that we can do it all ourselves. What a pickle we get ourselves into! One of Jesus's disciples, Peter, got himself into a similar pickle when he decided he could walk on water, like

In truth, we are building a very conniving muscle—the muscle of resistance.

Jesus. The incident can be found in Matthew 14, where we read of the disciples sailing a small boat across the lake of Galilee while Jesus ascends a mountain to pray. But the wind is against them, and they are battered by waves, making no headway at all. In the early morning, they spy a figure walking on the water. The disciples feel afraid, because they think the figure is a ghost. Jesus calls to his disciples, "Take heart, it is I; do not be afraid." Peter wants to be like Jesus, so he gets out of the boat and tries to walk on water. Peter takes a couple of steps with his sights set on Jesus. But as soon as he loses faith in Jesus's presence and becomes distracted by the wind, Peter sinks into the water.

See why it's so important to not do this alone? We all desperately need to be accountable to someone in our process, and we need the strength of many to get us through a hard time. We need partners who can help us build the muscles of action, rather than resistance.

Joan and her brother Ben were good friends growing up. Everyone noticed their teamwork, but the siblings always took it for granted. As adults they pursued their separate careers and went about their lives. One day Joan lost her job and couldn't find another one. Ben called Joan occasionally to see how she was faring during unemployment. Every time he did so, Joan told him she was baking cookies. Ben couldn't decide if cookie baking was a good or bad distraction for Joan, but he loved cookies so he dropped by to pay her a visit. Ben, a professional chef, tasted Joan's cookies and had an idea. He suggested that instead of eating her way through job loss, Joan could partner with him to market a new cookie brand. Joan needed her brother's skills as a chef and his compassion as a family member to help her turn cookie-baking procrastination into a moneymaking enterprise.

Is the goal of taming our resistance meant to imply that we should all know what we are doing as we search for a job? Absolutely not. How to deal with job loss is not something we really want to learn, so we don't typically figure out the steps until we have to. And the skills of job finding are inherent to very, very few people.

Here's the truth: when it comes to dealing with a job and seeking new employment, we learn by doing.

None of us likes to feel ignorant, so we let our wounded pride and naïveté further fuel our resistance. Here's the truth: when it comes to dealing with a job and seeking new employment, we learn by doing. Sort of like learning to read or learning to swim. We simply can't stay on the sidelines of life when life hands us employment challenges. We have to get off the couch and onto the playing field of mistakes and victories. What gets us through? Sheer perseverance, and faith that is practiced day by day through listening for God and remembering we are not alone. God invites us to focus on God's promises of presence and strength that embolden us to act. God's love is revealed in our failures and our faith.

To counteract resistance, we can try building our persistence muscles. We can learn from Helen, who made three calls a day for information interviews and took a course in something she always wanted to learn to get herself moving again.

> When anxiety was great within me, your consolation brought me joy.
> (Ps 94:19)

Prayer

God grant me the serenity to accept the things I cannot change, the courage to change the things I can, and the wisdom to know the difference.
—Reinhold Niebuhr, "The Serenity Prayer"[7]

Questions for Journaling

How did Jesus deal with losses in his life?

Write the prayers about your life that you most want God to hear.

Set a timer for ten minutes and use that time to write a list of to-do's you can accomplish. Each day extend the time by one minute.

Vulnerability

We pull up to a corner to wait for a traffic light. A man or woman stands there with a sign asking for help. We try not to meet the gaze of that person, but we still see them out of the corner of our eye. Many responses might cross our mind, such as pity, anger, or despair. However we feel and act, there's no doubt that we have been exposed to a vulnerable person and system. One of the reasons such encounters evoke such deep feelings in each of us is that we are also human, and therefore vulnerable.

Losing our job can undoubtedly leave us feeling bare and unprotected in the world. The structures, both literal and figurative, that we relied on to support our life turned out to be transitory. Will we too join the ranks in tents and tarps under the bridge, exposed to the world in ways we abhor?

Vulnerability is a very tender topic, so we need to be gentle with ourselves as we take stock of our newfound exposure. Ironically, vulnerability encases a core of power if our vulnerability can be shared. One of the most profound mysteries of our faith is that Jesus became vulnerable, and identified with the vulnerable, as a way of exercising the truest power.

Our connections to strangers and services will be strengthened in ways that affect us long after we find another job.

When we are slightly more honest and open about our need for others—and what is vulnerability other than a need for help?—we begin a new journey of learning to know a larger world. Our sense of judgment and our pat answers may be sacrificed along the way. Our connections to strangers and services will be strengthened in ways that affect us long after we find another job. Still, vulnerability can be hard to stomach for normally self-sufficient types. Face it, we always assumed we were taking care of ourselves.

Two Bible stories remind us of the costs and benefits of vulnerability. The first story comes from 2 Kings 5, where we read about the healing of Naaman the Syrian. Naaman has a big job—leading his country's army. He also has a big problem—he suffers from leprosy and is covered with sores. Naaman hears that God's prophet Elisha can heal him, so Naaman heads off to find this man of God. Elisha hears that Naaman was coming and sends him a message: go and wash in the Jordan River seven times to heal your leprosy. Naaman feels highly offended by this message; he expected Elisha to come in person to see such an important man. Naaman also can't understand how simply dipping in the Jordan River could bring about healing. Nevertheless, Naaman finally listens to his servants, who encourage him to heed the healing words of Elisha. Naaman literally lowers himself (seven times) to be healed. The water literally washes away his pride and restores his flesh. Naaman goes home praising and thanking God, healed of leprosy, blessed by vulnerability.

Sometimes we miss the chance to be rescued from our plight of joblessness, because we stubbornly hold on to old inklings of what will heal us. Our pride and narrow ideas can limit us, like they did for Naaman. Mark resisted taking a job that he felt was beneath him, because he worried about others seeing him in the new role. Finally, with his unemployment checks coming to an end, Mark agreed to the job. He resented the new work until one day at the grocery store Mark noticed how a friendly worker went out of her way to serve him. He realized that he could care less about the clerk's status; he just appreciated her customer-service skills and great attitude. Inspired by the clerk, Mark embraced his work and got on with life.

The second story comes from Mark 12, where the account of a widow's offering turns our ideas about vulnerability on their heads. In this scripture passage, Jesus teaches his disciples a lesson about humbling oneself to share and depend on God's grace. Jesus expresses disdain for a pompous rich man who called attention to his own actions. He praises a vulnerable widow, who shared her two last coins with others and became a quiet model of generosity. But, Jesus's disciples may have wondered, why would we choose to become so vulnerable? Jesus shows them that the widow put her life in the context of the lives around her. She displayed a sense of trust in what was beyond her. Seeing a bigger picture and trying out a deeper trust in God—these are possible gifts of vulnerability. It's no accident that vulnerability and generosity often go hand in hand. Our dependence on God leads us to recognize our interdependence with God's children, our neighbors.

> Let me abide in your tent forever, find refuge under the shelter of
> your wings.
> (Ps 61:4)

Prayer

O Lord, my heart is not lifted up,
my eyes are not raised too high;
I do not occupy myself with things
too great and too marvelous for me.
But I have calmed and quieted my soul,
like a weaned child with its mother;
my soul is like the weaned child that is with me.

O Israel, hope in the Lord
from this time on and forevermore.
—Psalm 131

Questions for Journaling

What have I learned about God and others during vulnerable times?

How does the story of the widow's offering sound to me after job loss?

Who is waiting for me to share my vulnerability?

Where can I look to find mentors like the widow in the Bible?

Hopelessness

Perhaps hopelessness will strike when you send out your twentieth job application and hear nothing back. Perhaps hopelessness will seep in when your child brings home a field-trip form with a hefty registration fee. Hopelessness can often be kept about an arm's length away, but when it lands with a thud, we know it.

The book of Lamentations provides an ideal example of God's people feeling and expressing their hopelessness. This book was written after Jerusalem was destroyed by the Babylonians in the sixth century BCE. After the destruction of their homeland, God's people cried out in five poems of lament for their physical, mental, and spiritual suffering. When we want to find words for our raw emotions and grief, Lamentations offers many such expressions of hopelessness:

> For these things I weep:
> My eyes flow with tears:
> For a comforter is far from me,
> One to revive my courage;
> My children are desolate,
> for the enemy has prevailed.
> (Lam 1:16)

Ironically, the wailing of God's people is paired with expressions of trust in God. This combination reminds us that glimmers of hope shine through, even in the bleakest of times.

> But this I call to mind,
> And therefore I have hope:
> The steadfast love of the Lord never ceases,
> His mercies never come to an end;
> They are new every morning;
> Great is your faithfulness.
> (Lam 3:21–23)

Lamentations serves as a model of pouring out our hurts to God, yet not equating our troubles with God abandoning us.

We do our best to stay one step ahead of hopelessness so as to remain positive for those around us. Maintaining regular routines,

There's a type of prayer called the welcoming prayer, in which we actually invite in the feelings that we usually shun.

putting ourselves in social situations, and having coffee with friends and neighbors can all help us outpace the hopelessness that nips at our heels and threatens to bring us down. We are understandably afraid of getting stuck in a morass of hopelessness, so we remain intent on "doing something."

One counterintuitive possibility is that the "something" we need to do is to welcome our hopelessness. Come again?! Yes, it's true. There's a type of prayer called the welcoming prayer, in which we actually invite in the feelings that we usually shun. Asking hopelessness to join us for tea sounds a shade self-defeating, but the other guest at the table is God. We dare to sit with hopelessness, just for a while, to consider what this feeling could teach us. And after we fully feel the feeling, we give it to God. It's not magic or easy, but the practice of welcoming prayer can be a much more enlivening way to deal with our hard feelings than running away from them and forgetting that God wants to be involved.

We never know what God will provide, but we believe that God will always be with us, no matter how desperate the situation. And somewhere in the back of our mind, as we thumb through Scripture looking for stories to help us, we remember: Ah yes, Jesus was a healer. Miracles that banish hopelessness did exist and still can happen. For example, in Luke 5 there is the story of a group of four friends whose buddy suffers from a condition of paralysis. (That's how hopelessness feels, doesn't it?!) The four friends risk believing that Jesus could heal their friend. But how to get their friend to Jesus? When Jesus is visiting a nearby house, they try bringing their paralyzed friend in through the door. Nope, too crowded. So they come up with another solution; they go up on the roof, cut a hole, and lower their friend down. In the end, Jesus heals the paralyzed man. Jesus also heals many others in the story. The four friends are healed of their hopelessness by creating a new vision and focusing on their end goal. The other people present are healed by watching faith in action.

Losing a job forces us to do things in new ways. The old motions simply won't work anymore. Awkwardly, painfully, we take stock of our "new normal" and fashion updated ways to get what we need, to keep moving forward.

The Smith family struggled with hopelessness after the factory closed where Dad Smith and his son worked. They scoured job sites for other places to apply, but any openings they discovered required advanced technical skills. Knowing that there were others in their community struggling with the same dilemma, the Smiths talked to their pastor and church elders about devising a solution. The church contacted a nearby community college and asked to enroll several of their members in a retooling program. Each morning the church van drove off to the college, filled with eight members taking technology courses. Each evening the same eight students gathered at church to study and to boost each other's confidence. The power of collective hope proved too strong for the despair of solitary hopelessness. The whole experience brought the Smith family to their knees, their church, and their neighbors.

> May your steadfast love, O Lord, be upon us, even as we put our hope in you.
> (Ps 33:22)

Losing a job forces us to do things in new ways. The old motions simply won't work anymore.

Welcoming Prayer

Dear God, I cannot change this feeling I have of hopelessness, so help me to trust that you can work through all things, even my despair. Amen

Questions for Journaling

Who are my creative friends who would be willing to help me find healing?

How is God calling me to welcome this situation of unemployment as a gift?

Do we just "Pollyanna up" and say thanks all day, in spite of our realities?

How can I share the truth with my family without unduly frightening them?

Where do I see miracles happening in our world today?

Gratitude

There's a lot of talk about gratitude lately, because our society needs this powerful tool to counteract the negativity around us. Still, gratitude possesses a reputation of being namby-pamby, doesn't it? And what we should be grateful for during days of uncertainty about our livelihood is not at all clear. Do we just "Pollyanna up" and say thanks all day, in spite of our realities? Well, yes, as a matter of fact.

Gratitude is not about saccharine words on a card; it's about finding the thing that gets us off rock bottom. When we really, truly don't see any way out of the trouble we are in, we are reduced to tiny, tiny actions that reframe our thinking. Gratitude can be the lifesaving action we rely on at that moment to restore our lives. Can't say thanks for a job, because a job doesn't exist? Okay, say thanks for the next breath, for the family you love so dearly that you are worried sick. For the free internet at the library. For the neighbor picking up your child after school. You're right! There are millions of losses, all worth feeling and noting. There are also profound blessings that can humble us if we begin to notice the abundance. A distraction from despair? Perhaps. But wouldn't that be what we asked for in the first place?

How to say thanks . . . Turn around and go back, like one of the men with leprosy who are cleansed by Jesus in Luke 17. As Jesus walks toward Jerusalem, ten men suffering from leprosy call out to Jesus for healing. Jesus feels compassion for the ten and sends them to be healed. While all of the men are thrilled by this outcome, only one man understands that part of his healing is to connect with his healer. One of the hidden blessings of job loss can be a new awareness of all the things we have been given and of the One who gave these gifts. While our healing may not be as dramatic as going instantly from illness to wellness, when we begin to look for God at work, we will be surprised by the subtle changes going on in our lives.

The most profound way to give thanks to God is to serve God. When we show our willingness, God always shows us work to do (volunteer or paid employment) and empowers us to pass on God's message of love and forgiveness. Nearly one hundred years ago, Pastor Otto Karlstrom and Alva Karlstrom made an interesting job move. Although they enjoyed a secure position at a thriving church, the Karlstroms chose to leave that job and start a mission for seafarers along Seattle's waterfront. They welcomed sailors coming to port with a place to shower, meet others, worship, receive mail, and gain job skills. They called the mission Compass Center, because Otto loved the sea and believed that our faith guides us.

A century later, Compass Center still exists to care for and empower people who need the same things they did from the start—a place to shower, meet others, worship, receive mail, and gain job skills. Nancy moved into a Compass shelter when living on the streets became too dangerous. There she met people who helped her turn her life in a new direction. She went back to school to finish college and study social work. Eventually Nancy joined the Compass staff. Her firsthand knowledge of clients' lives and work issues made her the perfect person to instill a combination of rules and mercy in her program. Nancy's thanks undoubtedly brought joy to God's heart, as her gratitude did to so many other hearts.

Pastor Terry discerned that God was calling him to start a Christian-Muslim initiative called Neighbors in Faith. He still has to seek out grants and find funding for this work, but business is booming. Churches are lined up with requests for Terry and his Muslim co-presenter to come and teach how to build faith relationships and shared ministry.

O give thanks to the Lord, for he is good; his steadfast love endures
  forever!
(Ps 118:1)

Prayer

You are the peace of all things calm
You are the place to hide from harm
You are the light that shines in dark
You are the heart's eternal spark
You are the door that's open wide
You are the guest who waits inside
You are the stranger at the door
You are the calling of the poor
You are my Lord and with me still
You are my love, keep me from ill
You are the light, the truth, the way
You are my Savior this very day.
—Celtic oral tradition, first millennium[8]

Questions for Journaling

Write a letter or poem of thanks to God.

Write notes of thanks to people who have recently helped you.

In what ways am I willing to be empowered by God to serve
others?

Summary

In this chapter we focused on eight feelings that come with
job loss—fear, shame, relief, confusion, resistance, vulnerability,
hopelessness, and gratitude. We surfaced stories from the Bible and
modern life to illustrate these emotions. Now it's your turn to
identify additional feelings you are going through that we haven't
named here. You can continue to write this chapter by naming your
feelings, finding stories of other people who have felt the same

things, combing through the Psalms, and writing your own prayers. May God bless and keep you along your path of life.

Resources

Schneider, Pat. *How the Light Gets In: Writing as a Spiritual Practice.* Oxford: Oxford University Press, 2013.

• A valuable book to learn about journaling and writing.

"Welcoming Prayer." Contemplative Outreach. https://tinyurl.com/y74966qt.

• Teaches us to welcome God into all parts of our life.

Wingren, Gustaf. *Luther on Vocation.* Eugene, OR: Wipf & Stock, 1957.

• Offers a comprehensive study of Martin Luther's ideas.

2
Thinking about Why We Work

MANY OF us work simply because work provides for our basic human needs. In other words, we work in exchange for capital that buys food, shelter, and healthcare, among other things. Jack approaches his work with this understanding. He puts in his forty hours and then forgets about work while he hunts and fishes on the weekends.

For others of us, though, work also transcends our basic human needs. Work equips us with gifts and benefits that surpass the necessities of survival. Work also gives us stimulation, balance, and the sense of purpose we need to feel alive. Georgia approaches her work with this type of mindset. She owns a hair salon and thrives on making her customers look and feel better.

Nearly all of us must work to live; some people also live to work. So how did the notion of work get started? From a spiritual perspective, we can go back to the creation stories in the Bible to find the "genesis" of work. From day one in the creation of the world, we read, God worked. God labored to bring something into being that previously did not exist—the universe. In the stories about creation in Genesis, we could say that God even followed a sort of "business plan." On each consecutive day, God fulfilled an agenda of creation and ticked off the tasks of systematically setting the heavens in motion and populating the earth with birds, animals, plants, and people. As the "week" of creation drew to a close, maybe God even shouted, "Thank God it's Friday!" Scripture tells us that after God completed the creation tasks, God ushered in the first Sabbath with a day of rest. We can easily note the similarities between God's workweek and ours—first we toil for a designated period of time, then we rest.

As part of God's creation efforts, human beings were introduced into the world. Initially, we were charged with the most basic work tasks—like finding food each day, laboring to deliver offspring, and worshipping God. Then, over the course of history from Genesis on, humans' work tasks became further delineated to ensure that the needs of larger communities were met. It only made sense that not everyone should or could do everything that was needed in the village or the city-state. So blacksmiths took up their particular trade and farmers got better and better at feeding people. As societies further developed, more and more needs arose and more and more jobs unfolded. Later still, rudimentary tasks became mechanized and leisure time expanded. Later, work evolved from merely being a means of survival to being an expression of one's gifts and talents. The phenomenon of reflection on work was born, as words like *vocare* (vocation) entered the vernacular.

During these vast sweeps of history, religions also developed, and teachers and followers reflected on our work for and with God. People laid out ideas about our relationship to God and God's desires for all of us, including God's vision that our lives would be enhanced by work.

> Nearly all of us must work to live; some people also live to work.

What Is Vocation?

The word *vocation* means "call." As Christians, we believe God calls us to a life of seeking and serving God. Martin Luther taught that we have vocations in four arenas: family, work, community, and church. At different points in our lives, one or another might take precedence. But we are called to serve our neighbors in all these places. Luther elaborated on the idea of vocation when he preached that every person is "called," not just priests and other clergy. Luther referred to the "priesthood of all believers," respecting each of us as being called by God to carry out God's work.

As we have seen, our need, compulsion, and desire to work harken back to the beginning of time and have been shaped by billions of people since then. So it makes perfect sense that when we are robbed of the opportunity to work or of the wages work provides, our grief, despair, and dismemberment tap into the whole history of human toil and labor.

Why do we work? Work includes purpose, structure, creativity, teamwork, the common good, legacy, beginnings-middles-ends, labor, sacrifice, and God-given gifts . . . among other things. Hopefully, this survey will spur other thoughts in each of us about why we work and why losing work shakes us to our core.

Work Provides Purpose

On a rural path near a country village in West Africa, I cross paths with a woman who is a farmer. She walks gracefully, like the other women in the village, and wears a colorful dress. We notice each other for many reasons, including, perhaps this one: I have a baby in my arms; she has a baby on her back. We smile and greet one another with a simple traditional hello. The farmer carries a basket on her head with millet she has harvested from her small plot of land to feed her family. The grain will be pounded and cooked to nourish children and adults. All day long in the hot sun, she has hoed and tended her crops.

I wonder as I continue my walk, what does the woman I passed think about while she works her land each day? How does she contemplate the meaning of God's creation as she works outdoors for many hours? That's what I get paid to think about during my workday. My work as a pastor is to dig up meaning in scriptural texts and attempt to feed people's souls. Two women's lives and sense of purpose cross on the red soil of an African path. While we are different, we share a need, and undoubtedly a desire, to work.

Each of us, the farmer and I, find a sense of purpose through our labor. Whether we're feeding our children or restoring a soul, work

> Two women's lives and sense of purpose cross on the red soil of an African path. While we are different, we share a need, and undoubtedly a desire, to work.

can provide a sense of purpose that focuses and energizes us to show up—again and again and again.

Finding our purpose makes us feel alive. God invites each of us to ponder the mystery of what we have to offer during our lifespan and to experiment with ways to improve the world. Maybe that impact is as clear as continuing traditions that have withstood centuries; maybe it's a new way of framing ancient ideas so that others can find and be led by holy truths.

Sometimes someone else determines the purpose for our work, and we are merely necessary labor fulfilling another's dreams. For example, we may work in a factory assembling mascara wands or truck parts and feel no inherent sense of purpose in the task. In that case, our purpose may be pared down to simply earning money or holding on to job security or building our experience—all of which are valuable reasons to work!

If finding purpose in work turns out to be a privilege that is not afforded us, we may search for purpose in unpaid work or avocations. Ideally, though, our work is aligned with the talents and gifts that were instilled in us from an early age. By practicing those natural-born affinities, we rest in a deep sense of purpose about our work.

Losing Work Means Seeking Renewed Purpose

When we lose our jobs, we suffer from a sense of lost purpose. We resent days of unemployment because they feel wasted. We're sometimes not even sure of our purpose. At night we go to bed unsure whether we accomplished anything that day. One way to renew our sense of purpose is to remember that as Christians our work includes discipleship. What is discipleship? God calls us as disciples to serve others and witness to Christ's love and forgiveness, no matter what career we pursue. Even when we are unemployed, God is calling us to serve in our family, community, and church. Discipleship is our spiritual job, our holy purpose—the job that

God invites each of us to ponder the mystery of what we have to offer during our lifespan and to experiment with ways to improve the world.

Even when we are unemployed, God is calling us to serve in our family, community, and church.

> How would you describe the purpose in your work?
>
> Do you work to live or live to work? Why?
>
> When have you practiced love and forgiveness at work?
>
> Are you surprised to be called a disciple? Why or why not?

God hired us to do and that God knows about without us ever listing it on our resumés. That's a purpose we can never lose.

Work Provides Structure

Before the beginning of civilization, during the era when people survived through hunting and gathering, work defined the structure of one's days. Task after task had to be completed. For example, babies needed to be fed. Fires had to be tended. Shelter had to be found or constructed. Work kept one busy; it also ordered one's days. Back-breakingly so, in fact. From sun-up to sundown, one was constantly busy trying to stay alive. Look at the birds in your backyard, or the squirrels in the park—that's kind of what work was like in those early days. Foraging for food and finding safety for the night.

Thankfully, we who live in homes and go to the grocery store for food don't typically have quite the number of labor-intensive tasks as our forebears (or as birds and squirrels). But there's a thread that still connects us to those hunter/gatherers. And that thread is the structure of work and the way it brings order to our days. More recently, our grandparents may have worked on farms, and so may we. The animals that need milking, the crops that need planting, and the land that needs tending all require a structure of must-do's to guide us and work to keep us on track.

With eons of structured work as our foundation, we can feel especially disconcerted by the lack of structure in jobs ushered in during our modern electronic age. For example, workdays are no longer always relegated to particular times and places. Young college graduates are happy to score jobs, but many of them soon find out that their bosses assume they are available 24/7. As long as they have a phone, they can be "on the clock." It becomes more and more confusing for them, as well as the rest of us raised in a different system, to sort out what is work and what is time off. But even modern work practices that seem to bleed all over everything are preferable to the shock of unemployment. Our empty days don't provide any of the structure for which we long.

When I think of structure, I'm reminded of a swimming pool. Along with my friends at the pool, I swim multiple laps back and forth across the water every morning. It's part of the work of our day—getting exercise, participating in a sustained activity that satisfies our brains, and sticking with a task even when we are tempted to stop. When we go to the pool for lap swimming, there are lane lines stretched across the water to help keep people sorted out and swimming in a formation. Those lines are like the structure of work. One doesn't jump into a pool with no lane lines and swim randomly here and there (unless you're a kid, of course—they can make the work of exercise just look like fun). The lane lines of work create limits for our time and organization for our lives. This enables us to relax—knowing that the boundaries are set.

Losing Work Means Creating New Structure

When we lose our jobs, we lose a valuable sense of structure that orders our days. Paula felt that loss of structure when she became unemployed. Before Paula lost her job, she felt like there were barely enough minutes every morning to get the kids fed and lunches made, and to hustle everyone to the car. After Paula's company informed her that she was laid off, she felt completely untethered by the lack of structure. During early mornings she was still able to focus on the tasks at hand, but after Paula dropped off her kids at school, she felt lost and didn't know what to do with herself. At first the experience of unemployment had felt a bit like a welcome break or a surprise vacation. Paula met friends for coffee or went

Young college graduates are happy to score jobs, but many of them soon find out that their bosses assume they are available 24/7.

How much structure do you need in your work and life?

When your structure falls apart, who helps you rebuild it?

What do you miss or not miss about the structure of working?

When can you set aside regular time in your day for prayer?

to the gym. But money worries quickly crept in and the feeling of not knowing what to do next wasn't far behind. For years, work had provided the structure Paula relied on without her ever knowing it. She had a desk, a boss, a lunch hour, clients, and a place to hang her coat. Suddenly all of that disappeared, and she found that she missed her well-constructed days as much as she missed the paycheck.

Realizing how much structure meant to her, Paula intentionally strove to build structure into her children's lives during her job search. She consistently honored their homework times and bedtimes, and kept up the regular visits to grandparents on the weekends. Paula continued to keep the structure of prayer in her life. Each day she gave thanks to God that she didn't have to worry about moving her children to a different home. She asked God to help her keep family routines going and not slide into despair.

Work Provides Creativity

Whether we're designing software, teaching preschoolers, or leading a church choir, work can tap into our creative side. We name God the Creator and believe that God was and is still at work unfolding the world we live in. As people of faith, we also declare that we are made in God's image. Which means each of us has been granted by God some ability and desire to be creative, to work as a creator in some way or another.

Bob consciously used his creativity on his job, which might seem surprising to us because Bob worked as a cashier at a big box store. But Bob intentionally created a welcoming relationship with each

> Each of us has been granted by God some ability and desire to be creative, to work as a creator.

customer who came through his line. Over the years, Bob found that he could quickly size people up as they approached his cash register. There were the customers who seemed eager to talk, and they were easy because Bob loved to talk. Then there were the customers who just needed a friendly hello or question about the weather or sports to break through their chilly façade. Because of his experience at reading people, Bob knew enough to leave some customers alone and just perform his cashier duties. He trusted that quiet respect could also lay the groundwork for later communication. Over the years, Bob got to know his customers, and many intentionally sought out his line for his kind spirit and efficiency. When the retailer downsized and Bob was asked to retire early, he grieved the loss of his relationships at work. Once in a while, he saw one of his old customers working at the library or bank, and they generously gave him back the welcome that he had creatively extended to them.

Often we equate creativity with jobs in the arts. But the creative nature of work can satisfy both artists and nonartists alike. When work taps into our desire to find new ways to do what we do better, that's creativity. For example, more effective lesson plans that help kids learn to read, better nursing care that prevents falls, and improved customer service that cuts down wait times—all of these goals can force us to unleash our creativity as we solve the problems. And this release of creativity can actually give us more energy for work. Creativity, in many cases, *is* the energy of work. A creative drive delivers us from same-old, same-old into new ways of waking up our brains and spirits, and gives us ownership over ideas that we generate.

Losing Work Means Creating New Solutions

Isn't it a relief that God shared the gift of creativity with each of us and entrusted us to keep creating the world around us? Creativity not only enlivens us during our work years; it also helps us think of fresh answers during periods of change. When we lose a job, for example, or get moved to another department that we don't like,

We name God the Creator and believe that God was and is still at work unfolding the world we live in.

> When you hear the word *creative*, what do you think?
>
> Think of a time when you had to "find a way where there was no way."
>
> In what ways has God made you a creative person?
>
> Who do you think of as creative?

our creativity can be the essential skill that keeps us from completely going under. Creativity, after all, is about finding new paths where there were none before—"finding a way where there's no way," as they say. That's exactly what we need to do when life throws us a curve ball such as unemployment or a toxic work environment. Maybe we can't solve everything with a creative attitude, but we certainly feel stuck and defeated without one.

Work Provides Teamwork

Each afternoon when he arrived for his afternoon shift at the sandwich joint where he had worked throughout high school, Trevor hung up his jacket in the back room. He put on the dopey hat he was required to wear, said hello to his buddies and the manager, and headed over to his workstation. Soon Trevor was staffing his part of the operation—constructing sandwiches with meat, veggies, and condiments at his station. When sandwich orders were called out, Trevor acknowledged what he heard and filled the hours with the work he knew so well.

Without Trevor, or someone in his spot, the restaurant where he worked couldn't function efficiently. Drinks Guy, French Fries Guy, Drive-Through Order Guy—all had to carry out choreographed tasks in order for the business to feed hungry customers. Trevor may not have realized that he was a cog in a well-oiled machine and would eventually want out of that setting. But for the moment he demonstrated one of the key elements that work is made up of—teamwork.

Teamwork can provide us with friendships, shared purpose, and the joy of collaboration. But however well a team works, job loss typically gets imposed on individuals rather than teams. After job loss, we can only sit at our computer wondering where the French Fry Guy is who always encouraged us to get our piece of the action completed. As we sit in a chair at the unemployment agency waiting to be seen, we may look around and wish that all the strangers around us could be the Drive-Through Order Guy, part of our old well-oiled machine. Instead we seem like parts scattered on the floor, waiting for assembly ourselves.

Among the ironies around us is the fact that in our increasingly globalized world, we experience more and more disconnects from our neighbors. Therefore, we treasure putting our heads together at work to fulfill common aims that transcend divisions. Work can actually be a relief from the contentiousness in our society that we don't know how to fix. At least Trevor could fix a sandwich and a meal with his coworkers. They could put aside their own selves and opinions in service to a boss, a company, and a customer.

From the time we are born, we depend on others and fit into one type of family system or another, adding our piece to the mix. In many jobs, our interdependence may not be as obvious as in other jobs. Our bosses and coworkers may work in totally different locations, or we may feel lost in a large corporation. Nevertheless, our efforts coordinate with others, even if those others seem to be invisible.

Losing our job often means losing our role as a member of a team with a common goal. Being off the team means mourning the security of working for an established company or the camaraderie of building an end product together with coworkers. While we may never know it, after we leave, our presence is missed on the assembly line, in the surgical suite, or at the port where we unloaded ships. Other team members depended on us for our contribution, and another team will depend on us again when we find a new job someday.

> We treasure putting our heads together at work to fulfill common aims that transcend divisions.

Losing Work Means Finding New Teams

Whether or not we practice teamwork, we were built for it. From the beginning, God envisioned a world in which we work together and care about the common good. Jesus demonstrated how to work with a team of disciples and break down barriers between people. In God's eyes, our work always includes looking out for one another and caring for the "least of these," and our personhood includes being in relationship with others. God would be happy to work with us to help us find new teams. In fact, God needs our teamwork to help solve the injustices in our world. When we go to church and worship, we practice the teamwork of praising, confessing, singing, and praying for our neighbors. When we sew with the church quilters, deliver food boxes with the outreach committee, and volunteer to be a lector, we partner with others through a sense of community.

Work Provides for the Common Good

When we lose our jobs, we first worry deeply about our own survival and the well-being of our friends and family. That's very natural. The renowned children's television personality Mr. Rogers said that in any natural disaster or family crisis, kids will first wonder, "What does this mean for me?" It seems that we never quite outgrow that stage of being afraid for our own safety and future.

But we are also grown-ups, and therefore we are capable of recognizing that unemployment isn't all about us. We worry about other people beyond our tight circle of family and friends. Work

> Whether or not we practice teamwork, we were built for it.

means seeking a common good for all parts of society. At times, we contribute to the common good to others. Social workers, job-placement services, and counselors work specifically to ensure that all of society hums along in a healthier way—to the benefit of all. At other times, we are the beneficiaries of the common good, and others have to help us. Our pride will undoubtedly suffer when we become the receivers of services that we didn't "earn" or "deserve." But our understanding of why and how people serve others, along with our humility and gratitude, can deepen in the process.

We may incorrectly assume that a political party or church denomination dreamed up the notion of the common good. In truth, the common good represents God's vision for humanity. We read about God's vision in our holy texts. In the Old Testament (Lev 19:18) and the New Testament (Mark 12:31), God's greatest law is laid out: Love your neighbor as yourself. And in Christianity, as well as in other world religions, we try to follow a simple, moral principle called the Golden Rule that illustrates God's vision for us: do to others what you would have them do to you (Matt 7:12).[1]

Some jobs clearly contribute to the common good—such as teachers, pastors, librarians, and public health workers. Losing jobs that enabled us to serve others can feel particularly devastating, because we end up worrying for others' futures along with our own.

For example, after he was laid off, Patrick spent many sleepless nights worrying about the young people he counseled in the job-training program he ran at a community shelter. How would they move forward without the guidance and common sense he doled out in his employment classes day after day? Would his clients land back in dysfunctional situations without someone to monitor their progress? Patrick even considered volunteering at his old workplace, but he needed to spend his time finding paid work so he could support his family.

The common good includes all the jobs and systems necessary to keep a society running smoothly. All one has to do is to visit or live in countries that don't have efficient systems to appreciate the fact

Work means seeking a common good for all parts of society.

Our pride will undoubtedly suffer when we become the receivers of services that we didn't "earn" or "deserve."

that our system works surprisingly well. Postal workers deliver our mail, bank tellers know their jobs, health clinics function in sanitary conditions, and buses arrive relatively on time. Our work can contribute to a standard of life that each of us enjoys but probably takes for granted.

While it may seem simple to divide the world of work into organizations aimed at the common good versus for-profit corporations, the distinctions are not really so clear. As an illustration—many corporations designate money and time so that their employees can volunteer for community projects and improve their local environments. In fact, these opportunities can be a big draw to new employees and generate important bonds between people as they work on meaningful projects or mentor underserved communities. When workers are laid off and can no longer participate in these efforts, they feel the sting of regret at the "more" they could have done. That's a sting that needs healing.

By supporting the common good, we intentionally combat the common "ungood," meaning natural disasters and societal devastation. First responders, community organizers, and public defenders live with the satisfaction that in their work they have attempted to put right something that threatened to destroy countless lives. Work for these folks includes a vision of protection and well-being for those in dire need. When their jobs are jeopardized, so is a piece of their soul.

Losing Work Means Finding New Ways to Support the Common Good

Tanya racked up a hefty sum of student debt in law school, but she felt confident that her first job as a lawyer would provide her with enough income to pay off her loans. However, finding a job proved very difficult and the firm that finally hired her downsized a year later, letting their newest crop of lawyers go. Tanya reimagined her career and remembered that she liked the pro bono work she did in law school. She landed a job as a public defender and found that what she lost in income, she gained in satisfaction. Tanya served

How do your neighbors benefit from the work you did?

Why is volunteering sometimes easier to do than paid employment?

What other gospel verses and stories encourage us to care about the common good?

Which of your employers would understand the term "common good"?

the common good from a front-row seat in court and felt special compassion for her clients, knowing that she too was vulnerable to job loss and economic distress.

Work Provides Legacy

"The family business." Most of us have heard that term. It means that generations follow in the footsteps of ancestors to become lawyers, shoe-repair shopkeepers, public servants, or insurance salespeople. Work for these folks is tied closely to skills passed down, as well as expectations of businesses surviving across multiple generations. Thus work can be made of more than the skills, education, and experience necessary for doing the job. Work can be stepping into a larger environment in which family legacy and business mix in all sorts of ways.

But legacy encompasses goals that go beyond family business. Beth, an editor for a church publishing house, is attempting to leave a legacy by helping authors write books that can change lives. Any of us concerned with how our work will enhance future generations could be said to care about our legacy.

Many of us assume that we don't have a "family business" because we don't own a company or trade that we pass down from parents to children. But we can define the family business with broader strokes. For example, a parent may master woodworking as a hobby

Any of us concerned with how our work will enhance future generations could be said to care about our legacy.

When we view our work as legacy, and our jobs are suddenly cut off, we despair of bonds broken with past generations and missed opportunities to serve future recipients.

and pass on that penchant to a son or daughter. That child becomes open to working in a field that requires her to use her hands. Serving others, solving puzzles, being open to changing from career to career—all of these traits can be a sort of family business that is inherited by a next generation that isn't necessarily related to us by blood.

In medieval times, another type of "family" business sprang up, known as guilds. Merchants, craftspeople, and artisans formed associations to help one another learn trades, market their goods, and manage commerce. The guilds, which we may think of as precursors of modern unions, were created to ensure a steady flow of skilled labor.[2] It's worth noting that no one has ever wanted to face the uncertainty and pain of job loss! Therefore, both families and guilds tried to protect each other from insecurity and lack of work.

In our day, the term "guild" can be ascribed to a collection of individuals doing the same type of work. Frequently that work is freelance based, such as computer programming or editing. A guild can provide more resources for its members in the form of seminars and employment websites.

Losing Work Means Expanding into New Legacies

When we view our work as legacy, and our jobs are suddenly cut off, we despair of bonds broken with past generations and missed opportunities to serve future recipients. We realize once again how much work connects us to others, through the families we inherit and the families we create.

Frank and Susan literally inherited the family business, a small dairy farm. Each of these siblings used both the skills they learned growing up on the farm and the lessons they learned as business majors at college to keep the operation going. Unfortunately, their efforts ultimately failed due to the trend of small farms being bought by larger agribusinesses. Submitting to the loss of their farm and farmer jobs, as well as the end of a legacy, felt like a deep

What do you consider your work legacy?

What's the family business—formal or informal—in your family?

When you hear the word *guild*, what do you think or feel?

Why does legacy matter to people called to hand down their beliefs?

blow. They struggled with the sense of impermanence and grieved the lives they had expected to live. As part of her recovery, Susan was heartened by studying her family history and recognizing that earlier generations had faced painful setbacks and unexpected moves to other farms. She found hope in a broader legacy—the motivation and skills to start over.

The work of faith involves the legacy of passing on our beliefs to our offspring and newcomers. Rather than being laid off from our job as conveyors and teachers of God's love, we sometimes resign from this job because the tasks of evangelism and faith formation prove difficult. Like Susan, we can rely on our ancestors to show us how they used hard times to pass their faith forward.

Work Provides Story Arcs of Beginnings, Middles, and Ends

Most stories have what we call a story arc. The story begins with an introduction of the characters and setting. As the plot progresses, a main character faces a major challenge to their old way of acting or thinking. As the story unfolds, we ascend the story arc. At the top of the arc we wait in suspense, wondering how the character will resolve the situation. Just over the top of the arc, a resolution occurs when the character is either able to change or fails to meet a challenge. The final section of the story arc is about how the main character lives out the consequences of that peak decisive moment.

> The work of faith involves the legacy of passing on our beliefs to our offspring and newcomers.

All of us, as readers and listeners, have been schooled in the story arc. You can test this statement by recalling some of your favorite fairy tales and realizing that from the time we were children we heard this pattern repeated in the stories that were read to us. Bible stories also followed this template. We wondered: Would the Good Samaritan stop and help the wounded man? Would Mary and Joseph safely escape to Egypt with the baby Jesus? At church, school, and home the story arc shaped the tales we took in.

So what does a story arc have to do with the nature of work? Two things, actually.

First of all, as workers we live a sort of story arc each day. In little ways and bigger ways, our workdays are filled with situations, suspense, and resolutions. Surgeons step into operating rooms with unknown results. Restaurant owners flip the sign from Closed to Open and never know what their profits will be that day. Professors step into classrooms and await the surprising questions students may pose about their assigned readings.

Living the story arc of our daily work satisfies something deep in our bones that needs fulfillment. Each day we need to wonder and we need to be challenged to face decisions and ethical questions. When we are deprived of that process, we feel a lack that we cannot name.

Second, our story arc can become stymied through unemployment. We live in a world where work stories increasingly seem to end prematurely. Just when we get settled into a new profession, technology may overtake human skills and force an early ending. Or societal change can shockingly disrupt the plans we made for our ongoing livelihood. That's what happened for Herb, the manager of a small sporting-goods store.

All was going well with the arc of Herb's story for decades. He knew his business backward and forward and diversified when the market demanded change. But the plot twist that Herb didn't anticipate, and couldn't conquer, was the new tendency for customers to buy online. Sadly, Herb's small business succumbed to a trend that he saw other business owners face. But Herb's story arc didn't end there. He went on to work for a larger sports company whose sales reps he had gotten to know over the years. Herb's expertise about what customers wanted and needed, no matter where they got their goods, proved to be a boon for manufacturers.

Story arcs provide a way to view our work lives. We live out mini story arcs in our jobs and are thrust into larger story arcs when unemployment seems to rob us of the expected endings of our stories. But remember what we learned earlier, that in a classic story arc, the main character faces an unforeseen circumstance, and the rest of the story becomes about how the character reacts and responds to the challenge. During job loss, we're the main characters! Our story continues through our job loss to what we do next.

Losing Work Means Writing New Stories

We're never alone in our stories, even if we feel alone. God works through people and events, accompanying us through joblessness and hopelessness to new beginnings. This good news makes sense because of the way our faith story works. In church we proclaim the mystery of faith: Christ has died, Christ has risen, Christ will come again. Because of Jesus's resurrection, death never gets the last word. We live in hope that the end of one story ushers in the beginning of

> Story arcs provide a way to view our work lives.

> We live in hope that the end of one story ushers in the beginning of another.

How do you get from the unwanted end of a job to the beginning of a new story arc?

What challenges enlivened you in your work?

What has joblessness taught you about your faith?

When have you worried about new technologies jeopardizing your work?

another. We depend on God to give us the strength and foresight to write new stories.

Work Provides Labor

Work, for many people, includes physical labor. Whether this is good or bad depends upon whether such work is your choice.

Ying is new to the United States. After she emigrated from China, she searched for a job in her field of business sales. Although Ying was quite an accomplished businesswoman in China, her English skills were lagging. The only job Ying could land was to work fourteen hours a day as a hotel maid. Carrying heavy sheets and cleaning hotel rooms is exhausting work. In the evenings, Ying attends English classes to improve her language skills so she can apply for a less labor-intensive job.

Ying's friend, Josef, also hopes to trade in his physical labor job for something less physically demanding. All day long he hauls suitcases back and forth on the airport shuttle he drives. His company also schedules him for weekends with no advance notice. Josef worries that his back will be injured by this hard job. Without health insurance or the safety net of worker's compensation, he recognizes that his situation is very precarious.

On the other end of the spectrum, there's Kaylin, who loved her physical labor job. She tried a desk job but hated feeling so sedentary. So Kaylin went back to school to become a physical therapist. Her new job allowed her to keep moving herself and encourage others to recover from operations and improve their own mobility. At the end of each workday, Kaylin felt the physical satisfaction of a job well done. When the healthcare provider for whom Kaylin worked merged with another system, though, there were too many physical therapists. With little seniority, her job was eliminated. During the weeks when Kaylin looked for new employment, one of her toughest struggles was sitting at a computer

> Work, for many people, includes physical labor. Whether this is good or bad depends upon whether such work is your choice.

How are you taking into account your need for physical or mental labor in your job search?

Look around today at all the people doing physical labor who serve each of us. What prayers can you pray for them?

Who has God provided for you to talk to about job loss?

How is the way you work different from your ancestors?

all day sending out resumés. She still needed the physical pleasure of work.

Back in the day, most workers relied on their bodies more than on their minds. These days that equation has flipped, and there are more desk jobs than physical labor jobs. But office workers have discovered that their bodies still need to be involved in their work. Standing desks have been invented to guarantee that we don't sit all day. Treadmill desks help workers attempt to keep muscles active as minds do their thing.

Losing Work Involves Spiritual Labor

Whether our jobs involve physical labor, like Ying's, Josef's, and Kaylin's, or the mental labor of staring at a screen all day, when we lose our jobs, we endure the spiritual labor of grieving and regrouping. Spiritual labor means relying on our faith to help us get through our grief and muster up hope for finding fresh possibilities. We call these endeavors spiritual labor, because they feel as toilsome as work and as uplifting as a job well done. We included a whole chapter in this book (chapter 3) on an alphabet of spiritual tools, including conversations, prayer, Bible verses, service, and listening. The spiritual tools were designed to help us work our way through the rigor of joblessness. When we engage in spiritual labor, God remains at our side with comfort, encouragement, tenacity, and truth to empower us.

Work Provides a Call for Sacrifice

Did Joey ever plan to be a barista? No way. But his college loans came due after graduation and he had to find something quick. Does Thien want to deliver newspapers in the snow at four in the morning with an old car? Not exactly. But Joey and Thien do their jobs nevertheless.

Work can certainly involve sacrifice. We put our dreams in the bottom drawer and instead do whatever we need to do to survive and care for others. This was true for Raymond, who left a job he loved to return to his childhood home and take care of his mother, who had cancer. And it was true for Alexander, who drives a cab at night and does deliveries for an office supply store during the day so his family can make ends meet. We don't have to go very far to find people quietly making enormous sacrifices that are tied to their jobs.

Where do they find the motivation to make these sacrifices? Children and loan officers can each inspire prompt action, you might say. But there's something deeper. Love, fear, and grit all push us to make sacrifices. In the past few years, military personnel and first responders have received greater recognition for their sacrifices. This is long overdue. But what about parents of young children who often have to balance babies and employment? They are showing up at work each day with other lives in mind. We should recognize them somehow as well.

Sacrifices are sometimes bruising to our egos. Cindy used to be the head of her marketing department. Now a younger worker, whom Cindy hired, has become her boss. In order to continue at the company until she's old enough to retire, Cindy must swallow her pride and live with the disrespect her new boss shows her. Each morning when Cindy steps into the elevator, she wishes she could pick a floor other than the one where her desk is. But she makes the sacrifice somehow.

Love, fear, and grit all push us to make sacrifices.

Making sacrifices can be hard, but accepting sacrifices can be harder still.

All of these workers could teach us a lesson or two concerning "it's not about us." Work has forced them, or invited them, to get past themselves. That's not easy to do.

Losing Work Means Accepting Others' Sacrifices

Making sacrifices can be hard, but accepting sacrifices can be harder still. Jennifer's mother-in-law takes care of her grandchildren every day while Jennifer looks for a new job, in spite of the fact that Grandma suffers from rheumatoid arthritis.

José's neighbors take him out for dinner once a week and pay for the meals. Doug's old boss phones colleagues regularly to help Doug find a new position. Jennifer, José, and Doug have learned to gracefully accept help, even when they see others literally paying the price for them.

Learning to be a receiver, as well as a provider, of sacrifices changes our mindset. We realize that we can't "earn" our friends' good deeds. Their actions signify a free gift that is beyond our control. But not beyond our gratitude. We can thank those who make sacrifices for us by renewing our trust in the goodness of humanity and attributing this goodness to God's love in the universe. We draw closer to those who sacrifice for us by expressing our genuine thanks and promising to pay forward their actions someday when it's our turn to help another.

"Amazing Grace" stands out as one of the most beloved hymns of all time. We sing and love this hymn so much because we need to remind ourselves again and again to accept the gift of grace.

What sacrifices did your job demand of you?

Where did you find the grit to keep going?

How have you felt when others made sacrifices for you?

Who could use a thank-you note from you?

Allowing others to sacrifice for us and accepting that God loves us, no matter what, are truths that seem too good to be true. Yet God invites us to live into God's amazing grace and to measure our lives not just by what we can do but by what God can do through us.

Work Provides Ways to Share Our God-Given Gifts

Indeed, there are definitely lessons to learn from the sacrifices contained in work. But if work is all sacrifice, it will be all . . . work! And that's not the idea God had in mind when God endowed each of us with particular gifts for working and sharing.

When Wayne wakes up these days, his first thought is, "What will I do today?" Ever since retirement, Wayne has struggled to fill his time. He's still searching for a rhythm to his days and meaning in helping others, rather than simply reading the paper at home and bothering his wife. Retirement may be landing especially hard on Wayne because he absolutely loved his job. He worked for forty years as an engineer for a company that built airplanes. When he was a young child, Wayne constructed his own paper airplanes. His love for aeronautics sustained him through college and led him into the company that became his second home.

Recently, Wayne heard that some of his old buddies are volunteering as docents at the aviation museum in his city. That idea has begun to sound better and better with each empty passing day. Wayne feels nervous that he would have to deal with unruly schoolchildren as a museum docent, but at least he would have a reason to get out of bed.

Ideally, we would all have the same problem as Wayne—that we loved our jobs so much that they centered our lives and kept us physically and spiritually fed over many years. That's what God wants for us. God, who created work in the first place, instilled special gifts and desires in each of us. It's no accident that we love what we love, and it's interesting that so many of the skills we possess became evident even when we were children. Think back

God, who created work in the first place, instilled special gifts and desires in each of us.

on some of the things you played as a kid. (Tag doesn't count!) Perhaps you baked cookies and grew up to run a bakery. Or maybe you were the one who always organized the neighborhood baseball games and you grew up to be a leader in your industry.

We don't have to live very long to recognize that people are gifted with specific skills, and enacting the work that comes most naturally makes us recognize what we've been exploring throughout this chapter—that work is more than work. Work is an education in living. Through work we discover purpose, structure, sacrifice, gifts, legacy, and the common good.

Losing Work Means Exploring Our Untapped Gifts

Every so often, we will see a friend in a coffee shop poring over a dog-eared copy of a classic book about job searching called *What Color Is Your Parachute?* When we see this book we get an inkling that our friend wants not just any job but the right job. Books like *What Color Is Your Parachute?* feature exercises in discernment, that is, exploring our inner talents and propensities and matching them with potential jobs and careers.

Thousands of years before *What Color Is Your Parachute?* was published, the Bible offered advice on discerning job skills. In Romans 12:6–8 we read, "We have gifts that differ according to the grace given to us: prophecy, in proportion to faith; ministry, in ministering; the teacher, in teaching; the exhorter, in exhortation; the giver, in generosity; the leader, in diligence; the compassionate,

Over the course of our lifetimes, as jobs come and go and our experiences build, we learn to unearth new gifts, take risks, and respond to the needs around us.

When did you work at a job that felt more like a pleasure than a burden?

What gifts do you notice in your children that you hope they will pursue someday?

Which of your gifts have surprised you as you've grown older?

If you could have any job, what would you choose?

in cheerfulness." The Bible never says that any of us get all the vocational or spiritual gifts. Over the course of our lifetimes, as jobs come and go and our experiences build, we learn to unearth new gifts, take risks, and respond to the needs around us. God blesses and weaves our gifts of wisdom and knowledge into different patterns—continually astounding us with opportunities to work and grow.

In this chapter we spent time dissecting work, to see what work is made up of. We did so to broaden our perspective on the nature of work and to name some of the things we lose when we lose our work. Whether we work to live or live to work, work provides us what God wanted for us in the first place—purpose, community, and avenues to use our special gifts. Understanding that we need these groundings can motivate us to keep trying to find new work that's authentic to who we are called to be. I wonder what answers this chapter has generated for you about why you work. I hope you will share your work reflections with someone who can help you get back to work—for many reasons!

Resources

Bolles, Richard N. *What Color Is Your Parachute?* Berkeley, CA: Ten Speed, 1970.

- A well-loved book for job seekers.

Craft in America. craftinamerica.org.

- A PBS video series that will spark your creativity by watching talented artists at work.

Center for Courage and Renewal. couragerenewal.org/podcast.

- Provides free podcasts by Parker Palmer on teamwork, leadership, and living into possibilities.

3

An Alphabet of Spiritual Tools to Cope with Job Loss and Job Search

EXPERTS NAME job loss as a grief similar to a death in the family. Therefore, we can't underestimate the depth of pain and disconnection that a person feels when they lose a job. One grief theory by J. William Worden suggests that there are specific tasks of mourning that need to be accomplished in order for grief to be completed.[1] These tasks are:

1. Accept the reality of the loss. Facing up to the truth that our job is gone and will not return is the first task that needs to be completed. Only when we accomplish this step will we be able to continue with our grieving process.
2. Work through the pain. Grief is painful, physically and emotionally. We don't need to imagine that there's something wrong with us because we feel so bad. That's part of grief.
3. Adjust to the new landscape of life. This may require adjusting to shifts in one's family, such as one's spouse suddenly becoming the main breadwinner.
4. Move forward. This step includes breaking new ground.

Completing these tasks will help us come to terms with job loss and return to a new state of normalcy. Involvement in support groups and grief counseling can help us move through these tasks.

In order to begin dealing with our grief and managing the persistent fears that come with job loss, we can also turn to faith practices to sustain us. Don't get me wrong. We all feel afraid, especially during times of unemployment. It would be strange if we weren't afraid! And completely banishing all our fears is not a realistic goal. But we can address our fear by using these tools so that anxiety does not entrap or paralyze us.

In this chapter we're offering you an alphabet of tools to choose from so that you can assemble your own spiritual toolkit. Many of these tools are undoubtedly present in our lives already. Nevertheless, they are valuable to name and define, because during a crisis we can feel very off-balance and distracted. Listing spiritual ways to get through and move ahead reminds us that God is present and wants to help us get through a difficult time.

A—Acceptance

We just read about the four tasks involved in dealing with grief, and the first one is to accept our loss. That's really hard, isn't it? We can easily spend a lot of our energy denying that we have lost our job. It's just so hard to get our head around the reality of something so difficult. Praying for acceptance means asking God to help us face the emptiness and go from there.

Please know that acceptance doesn't happen in the first moment one is laid off from a job. Nor does it occur on the first day or even the first week. Everyone is different, of course, as is every situation. Sometimes we are given warnings about upcoming layoffs or we gain an inkling as those around us are downsized. But when job loss finally taps us on the shoulder, we feel our heart drop and it's really painful to let the news sink in.

So how do we go about accepting this new and unwanted reality? The answer to that question is why this word, *acceptance*, begins our list of spiritual tools: we really need God's help to grasp the impact of job loss. So we take our situation to God in prayer. We will call out aloud or silently, "Please help me!"

The answer to our prayer may not come immediately or even very quickly. Still, we ask the God of abundance to hear our plea.

To begin dealing with our grief and managing the persistent fears that come with job loss, we can also turn to faith practices to sustain us.

Praying for acceptance means asking God to help us face the emptiness and go from there.

How do you know you have accepted or not accepted job loss?

What actions, small and large, have you taken to move ahead?

We can turn over the wave of fear and uncertainty to God, so that we don't have to be alone. Acceptance will typically creep in little by little. For example, we may be able to call someone in our family and admit our situation. Or we may find the courage to go to a website with job listings and begin the search process. God works in mysterious ways, but God really loves us and wants us to find a deeper sense of being provided for. Even brief moments of acceptance will make a big difference to combat our sense of denial. In those moments we will be able to say that something we didn't choose happened, yet we will be okay. The moments become a little longer or more frequent as the shock wears off and we regroup. But remember, acceptance is always a God thing. It's an invitation to recognize a bigger picture of God's love and care for our lives.

Also, acceptance doesn't mean rolling over and playing dead. Another *A* word is *action*. God's providence somehow combines with our actions in a way that brings healing and change. Here's an idea that can help us recognize our action steps, even when we feel stuck. Rather then simply make to-do lists (which are of course important), we can make lists of the things we've already done. Even small things. For example, we could include on the list that we talked to our kids about their feelings, prepared nutritious meals, prayed with our pastor, got a good night's sleep, and took a walk. Each of those actions may not seem significant, but they add up to consistency and care for others and ourselves.

B—Bible Verses

There will be days after job loss when our thoughts just spin with "what-ifs" and dire scenarios. It's easy for our minds to get stuck in these unhelpful ruts, especially when we are robbed of purpose, community, and structure. Therefore, we need a defense against

> God works in mysterious ways, but God really loves us and wants us to find a deeper sense of being provided for.

"monkey mind." We need something besides fear for our minds to focus on.

Beloved Bible verses can serve as an answer. They provide a mantra to which we can return again and again. The words serve as a handhold to which we can cling. When I worked as a hospital chaplain in a cancer center, I visited patients going through stem cell transplants. One day I walked into a room and met a patient who happened to be a pastor and had his Bible propped open on his bedside table. I asked him how his faith was helping him to get through his illness. Immediately the pastor answered, "Exodus 14:14." He went on to explain that this verse describes a moment when Moses and God's people have the Pharaoh and his army behind them and the Red Sea in front of them. The verse reads, "The Lord will fight for you; you have only to keep still." My friend invited me to share that verse with other cancer patients, and I did! I wrote it in cards and told others. The verse itself and the practice of holding on to one message proved helpful to many of the people I saw.

What are your favorite Bible verses to get you through hard times? This spiritual tool can be most effective if you search the Bible and find a verse that feels like it applies to you. The Psalms are a good place to start. In case you are not familiar with Psalms, it's a book in the middle of the Bible that looks like poetry.

"For thou art with me." (Ps 23:4).

"Be still and know that I am God." (Ps 46:10).

The promises of Jesus can also be a good source of peace. You can find these in the four Gospels: Matthew, Mark, Luke, and John. Here are some examples, but remember that the verses you find on your own will be the most meaningful for you.

"I am the way, the truth, and the life." (John 14:6).

"Come to me, all you who are weary and heavy-laden, and I will give you rest." (Matt 11:28).

What are your favorite Bible verses to get you through hard times?

"Peace I leave with you; my peace I give you." (John 14:27).

"I am the vine and you are the branches." (John 15:5).

"I am the light of the world." (John 8:12).

Memorizing a Bible verse works well because then the verse is always with us. In addition to memorization, we can type the verse into our phone or put a copy of the verse on the dashboard of our car, the refrigerator, or the bathroom mirror. We want to be able to see the help we seek during our daily lives.

C—Conversation (with Coffee)

Conversation is one of the first tools I offer because of alphabetical order *and* because talking to others is such a key spiritual strategy. God created us to be interdependent creatures. Therefore, when we go through hard times, we need to talk to someone, like our sister, our college friend, or our spouse.

Perhaps we'll have a hard time imagining that someone would want to hear our tale of woe.

Not that talking to someone is always our first inclination! Far from it. We may be tempted to isolate ourselves and lick our wounds for a very long, lonely time, because job loss can include feelings of shame and regret. Perhaps we'll have a hard time imagining that someone would want to hear our tale of woe. But when we put ourselves in another's shoes, we remember that of course we would want to try to help, and we can assume that others will want to help us.

Who to talk to? Our pastors and spiritual directors are especially trained to listen and are not at all surprised to hear from someone going through job loss. Our good friends and those with whom we can really be ourselves are also a good place to start. Job counselors also understand our process and have watched people go through classic stages of job loss and job search. They can keep hope alive for us because they already trust the process of grieving and finding new work possibilities.

> Where do you go to listen and talk to God?
>
> Who have turned out to be your most trusted friends?

Sometimes it's enough to just go for coffee or a walk with a friend and get out of our homes and heads for a while. Our conversations don't even have to be intense or profound. Simply hearing someone else talk or getting our minds off our own troubles can be a gift.

When we feel ready, we can share our deeper thoughts and feelings. These spiritual conversations include honesty about the situation and real questions about how to keep our spirits lifted. If we have conversations with people who make us feel ashamed of our predicament, who don't know how to listen, or who feed us platitudes—probably better to steer clear of them for a while.

Is it possible to have a conversation with God? I think so. At least I think it's really helpful to say out loud to God exactly what we think, feel, fear, and hope. That's a prayer, actually. God's side of the conversation can be harder to discern, but sometimes just hearing our own words spoken aloud is all that we need to truly understand our problem. Learning to understand God's language takes as much work as learning to understand a foreign language. The steps are surprisingly similar—spend time with God and listen very hard. Eventually we become a little more fluent in the language of faith.

D—Daily Devotions

The idea of adding, or reinstating, a devotion practice in our days may sound unrealistic, especially on top of everything else. But consider it, please, because devotions don't have to take a lot of time or require significant organization. Every denomination produces small devotion books or apps that do a lot of the preparation for us. We get to explore verses of the Bible and read some thoughtful words that a devotional writer has pondered.

> Simply hearing someone else talk or getting our minds off our own troubles can be a gift.

Alternately, we can read a couple of pages each day of a book or blog written by a spiritual writer. Such books, sermons, and blogs hold enormous power to reframe our lives. Henri Nouwen, Eugene Peterson, and Joan Chittister write about spiritual themes in very inviting ways that teach us about God and faith. We can even get these writings through our local library or download them onto our phones. Even a few words a day can keep us in touch with the faith center of our lives.

Our devotions can also include formal or informal prayers. Some people like prayers written by saints or spiritual leaders. We can rely on those and throw in prayers of our own. The amount is not as important as the daily practice.

Don't forget the power of silent prayer as a step in our daily devotions. It may seem counterintuitive to spend ten to twenty minutes in silence, focusing on our breathing and just being with God. After all, there are so many things to do. But that time pays off richly. When we spend time with God, we have the potential to realize that deep down, at the very heart of our lives, we are not alone. God is there with us. God will never abandon us; in fact God wants to hear exactly what we need. The beauty of such prayer is that for a span of time each day, we don't have to prove anything. Our only job is to sense our worth in God's eyes.

When we spend time with God, we have the potential to realize that deep down, at the very heart of our lives, we are not alone.

E—Exercise

Everyone tells us to exercise. We have heard before that exercise produces hormones called endorphins that literally make us feel better. Just like daily devotions, the practice will pay off through consistency. Exercise doesn't have to be long or complicated. A walk outside can really turn our spirits around in a short time. There's something about having all that air around us that makes us remember the universe is much larger than our little jail of self-absorption. This is what makes exercise a spiritual tool. When we walk, bike, run, or skateboard outside, we're in God's creation. God comes to us in new ways like autumn leaves, puffy clouds, and silent snowflakes.

Exercise also provides another spiritual gift—rhythm. After a few blocks, we get into a pace when we walk. That pace stills our minds. With our bodies busy and our minds stilled, our spirits are freer. Our souls get a rest from churning with worry or sitting around obsessing. God wants rhythm for our lives. God instilled in us the need for regular food and drink, work and rest, youth and adulthood. God designed these rhythms for our lives and livelihoods. The steady pace of our steps echoes the heartbeat of God's dreams for our lives.

F—Friends

Our friends are our friends precisely because we don't share only good news with them. We share bad news too. Acquaintances are important in our lives. But friends, on the other hand, are not just important. They are essential.

Friends can offer much healing for our souls during times of job loss. Most of all, friends can believe in us. This feat proves absolutely life-giving when we somehow lose the ability to believe in ourselves. Job loss can do that to us! Friends agree with us about how much our experience feels unfair and barely endurable. They also can disagree with us in good ways, such as challenging our

Friends, on the other hand, are not just important. They are essential.

Our friends want to be there for us, just as we want to be there for our friends.

What friends have you called?

What friends could you contact right now?

negative thinking. Friends have contacts; contacts mean networks; networks serve as a key way to find new work.

Our friends want to be there for us, just as we want to be there for our friends. We might worry that we will sound too needy to our friends. How many times can they hear that we are scared and lost? Lots of times, evidently. That's what makes them friends.

There's a reason that one of the most beloved hymns is "What a Friend We Have in Jesus." Because we haven't ever seen Jesus, it can be difficult to know how to describe him. The hymn writer Joseph M. Scriven chose his dearest illustration by comparing Jesus to a friend. He wrote the hymn in 1855 for his mother in Ireland, who missed him when he moved to Canada. Although none of our friends can match up to Jesus's power and love, our closest companions help us carry heavy loads. They are much more willing to help than we are willing to let them help. Often our pride gets in the way of turning to others. Swallowing our pride and realizing that we are all just human is another huge spiritual lesson.

G—Groups

We have just spoken of the enormous gift of friends who can listen and talk with us during job loss. Sometimes we need others who "are in the same boat." At that moment support groups can provide the solace, camaraderie, and inspiration we are lacking. There's nothing like being able to "tell it like it is." There's a sort of instant understanding among members of support groups. We can decipher in a few words what another is going through because we have been there. Those who truly understand each other's pain rarely judge one another.

> Where two or three are gathered in my name, I am there among them.

In Matthew 18:20, we read: "Where two or three are gathered in my name, I am there among them." Truly God is present among us. God came to our world in Jesus. God continues to arrive as a Holy Spirit who binds us together. The irony is that when we go through the hardest parts of life, we find ourselves feeling the closest to one another and to God. Vulnerability is the thing we avoid the most often, yet when very human hard times arrive, we build relationships founded on faith and real life.

So how do we find support groups to help us through job loss? Our answers to that question will vary, based on our community. Suffice it to say that finding a group involves seeking one diligently and not being afraid to keep asking whether one exists. Maybe we are the type of people whose gift, or need, is to start our own support group. Our faith communities are natural places to convene and nurture support groups. We are called to help one another and share our predicaments.

H—Health

Going through trauma is exacerbated when we suffer ill health. Our minds reflect the state of our bodies, and if we don't eat well, sleep enough, and exercise, we'll be "in a pickle." All of us know this, but living out the goal of taking care of our health can be quite difficult during stressful times. As we struggle to maintain decent habits, sometimes we forget to ask God for help with our mental and physical health. We name God as a healer, so why not take advantage of the Great Physician and pray for God's strength to take care of ourselves?

Taking care of our spiritual health deserves as much attention as our other health decisions. Tending to our spirit means keeping in touch with the sacred in our lives. We can do this through worship, prayer, music, silence, reading, writing, and reflection groups, to name a few resources. Our spiritual health can actually improve when we face a challenge such as job loss, because we are forced to draw closer to God for sustenance and to develop spiritual practices that order our days.

Sometimes it helps to look around and notice whom we would name as spiritually healthy. Someone we know may stand out as a person who clearly seems to understand what matters or who seems

Our spiritual health can actually improve when we face a challenge such as job loss, because we are forced to draw closer to God for sustenance and to develop spiritual practices that order our days.

to exude a contentment that could have only come from believing in fundamental truths. There's a good chance such a person, or people, will have undergone adversity and found answers through hard journeys.

Identifying and seeking out those people to walk with us can be one of the best investments in our spiritual health. If we broke our leg, we would want a skilled surgeon to set the bones so it would heal properly and we could walk again. When our hearts are broken by experiences like job loss, we need rock-solid spiritual companions who bring much-needed healing by walking alongside us and helping us trust in future answers, surprises, and grace.

I—Intention

Recent studies attest to the connection between writing down goals and achieving them. All of us would benefit by taking the time to define what we seek in a new job and intend for our future. We can also name our spiritual intentions that have been unearthed in the job-loss experience, such as, "I intend to be available to others in my faith community who go through an experience like mine."

There's also another spiritual meaning for the word *intention*. This perspective on intention originates from a theologian named St. Ignatius and can be very helpful during times of job loss. We all know how our thoughts can rampantly run to negative and unhealthy places during crises. It's natural, and even necessary, to go through times of resenting our old bosses, colleagues, or companies. Sometimes, however, we get very obsessed with those people and the wrongs we feel were done to us. It's hard to get past the resentment and redirect our energy for finding a new job.

St. Ignatius recommended to Christians that we assume the best intention in others. In other words, we pray to develop compassion, even for those who have thwarted our lives, and ask God to somehow reveal how God is working mysteriously through the intersecting of our lives with the lives of those people. If it sounds like only a martyr or saint could fulfill this practice of assuming the best intention, be assured that the process doesn't happen through solely our own effort. These ideas about intention would be a great topic to talk about with a pastor or spiritual director or to bring to a support group in a faith community.

J—Jesus

Jesus lived an itinerant life of preaching on the road, eating with strangers, and staying wherever someone would take him in. That lifestyle worked for the Savior of the world, but what about for the rest of us who crave more security and aren't the Son of God?! How does Jesus relate to our plight of feeling the ground shake beneath us when our jobs disappear?

The more appropriate question for this spiritual tool inventory is: How do we relate to Jesus? Losing our jobs often leads us to take another look at the additional job we endeavor to accept as Christians. That is the job of discipleship. As we get wrapped up in resumé writing and selling ourselves, we need the perspective of our faith journey to keep us grounded. Our faith reminds us that our lives are based on what God can do and does do, not merely what we can do. That miraculous surge of relief we feel when we get the call that says we're hired gives us a glimpse of God's grace. We find it absolutely thrilling and essential to find work, and even better to be fulfilled in that work. That's what God wants for us—to labor, find

> Losing our jobs often leads us to take another look at the additional job we endeavor to accept as Christians. That is the job of discipleship.

How do you stay connected to Jesus's message?

When have you had to deal with feelings of betrayal and resentment? How have you managed those feelings?

What God wants even more for us is to know that we are loved and treasured whether or not we have a job, and to believe in the promises that God provided for us.

meaning, and care for others. What God wants even more for us is to know that we are loved and treasured whether or not we have a job, and to believe in the promises that God provided for us.

One of the most important ways Jesus can serve as a resource for us is when we feel particularly rejected. Those times can be frequent during the experience of job loss and job searching. After all, the unemployment scenario is often painfully demoralizing. At those times we have a resource that may be gathering dust on our shelves. That resource is called the Bible. In the New Testament we can find stories of Jesus being rejected by his closest friends and society itself. We are followers of Jesus, the one who endured betrayal and won the day through love that was stronger than all that. Losing our jobs can help us be open to Jesus doing his job—leading us through a human experience he survived and overcame.

K—Kneeling

Of course we would assume that a list of spiritual coping mechanisms would include prayer. And we're right! Taking a knee before God can be just the exercise we need to ask for mercy, demand justice, and show our reverence.

There are other places to kneel besides our church pews and bedroom rugs, however. Here are two: We can kneel next to our children. First of all, to achieve eye-level with them and to see how they're doing. Kids completely feel the stress around them. Whether they respond by acting out or getting extra quiet while your family goes through job loss and changes, children are definitely sensing the tension in the air. Getting down to their level to play, read, talk, listen, and pray together each day will help kids find the time with you that they long for.

A second place to kneel is beside someone who is literally feeling down and out. Finding our place at the bedside of an invalid, at the sleeping mat of a homeless person, or next to a companion who is also going through job loss literally means leaning over and learning we are not alone. Our problems, which feel huge and are huge, are part of a bigger picture in which others suffer and need our compassion, whether or not we have employment.

Our hurts tie us to other hurts. When we reach out, we stop being distracted by our own issues and attempt to bring comfort and good news to others. In so doing, we proclaim a larger truth of love and demonstrate how alive we still are.

L—Laughter

All of this joblessness gets so heavy at times that we can barely breathe for all the seriousness in the room. That's the moment to watch the funniest show we can think of or get together with someone who always gives us a belly laugh. We can also go to a pet store and watch puppies frolicking, view silly cat videos, or dare to take ourselves less seriously by making crazy faces in a mirror. Go ahead—no one's watching!

Remember the story of Sarah and Abraham in the Old Testament? They were old folks who always wanted to have a baby. They waited about as long as we feel we are waiting for our next job. In other words, an interminably long time. Finally, finally, a miracle happens. Miracles do happen, you know! Sarah finds out she's going to have a baby. Well, someone tells Sarah that she's going to have a baby. And she does the only thing she could besides roll her eyes. Sarah laughs. We read in Genesis 21:6: Sarah said, "God has brought me laughter, and everyone who hears about this will laugh with me." Sarah laughs so heartily that the baby gets named Isaac—he who laughs.

Who makes us laugh? Our toddlers? The writers of hilarious greeting cards? Laughter may be the very last response we think we can conjure up during serious times, so we need to keep humor sources close at hand.

Laughter and tears are first cousins. Why else would we laugh so hard we cry? Or cry so hard . . . wait, that doesn't really work, does it?! At any rate, both powerful responses reach the bottom of the

Our hurts tie us to other hurts.

Laughter and tears are first cousins.

well of our feelings. That's a spiritual place. While we're there, in our laughter and tears, we might as well remember that it was at a well that God promised us living water.

M—Music

Research abounds these days about the power of music to heal us. Recently, music therapists collaborated with brain scientists to develop a program to treat Parkinson's disease with music. Patients who can no longer talk are actually able to sing and express themselves in ways that eluded them for years.

What's our playlist for the job-acquisition process? By that I mean, what music keeps our spirits up or centers us during the tedium of waiting and applying? Putting together a playlist can be a creative endeavor that focuses our spirit and intention. Do we need to hear the victorious theme of *Rocky*, the happy banjos of bluegrass, or the strength of a grand symphony as we summon up the courage to send out application after application? Music soothes, distracts, transcends, fulfills, and speaks a language beyond us. The music of liturgy can reach places in our souls our minds had no hope of reaching. Those places need to be tended. All the more reason for us to go to church and let music do its sacred work.

And if we are musicians, we can join the music teams of choirs and other groups. In these groups we find our musical voices, even if our spoken voices seem to have been muffled temporarily.

N—Naps

God's people have always been nappers. Which is a good thing, because in the Bible we find lots of stories about God visiting

Music soothes, distracts, transcends, fulfills, and speaks a language beyond us.

people during sleep. While sleeping, Jacob dreamed he wrestled with God at the river, and Pilate's wife dreamed that Jesus was innocent. Maybe when we sleep, God finds an opening to get into our hearts, rather than be shut out by our awakened sense of stewing and foreboding.

Sleeping all day to hide from unemployment? Bad idea. Catching a nap to make sure we are well rested and able to face the stress? Good idea. Back in the chapter on why we work, we recalled the creation story in which God created the universe in six days and rested on the seventh. There it is! Justification for a nap. But there's more. When we rest, we give God a chance to work. The task of finding new work doesn't all depend on us. If God could create mosquitoes and day lilies, God can also help us fashion a fresh future. Our "job" is to remember to go to God as a source of perseverance, help, and even miracles.

Sound like a good idea? Sleep on it.

O—Openness

Planning gives us back a sense of some control after we have suffered from feeling out of control. In fact, being a planner gives us something to do in the interim between jobs. We can plan updates to our LinkedIn page, list potential employers, connect with old colleagues, and design a new business plan. Planning keeps us from merely spinning in confusion or going backward in despair. If we hire a job coach, that person will work with us on planning next steps and outlining processes.

To balance all that planning, we can practice openness. Each day situations and opportunities arise that invite us in. Our intuition

Sleeping all day to hide from unemployment? Bad idea. Catching a nap to make sure we are well rested and able to face the stress? Good idea.

Openness means being curious about what God might be up to in the universe and being willing to take a risk in the name of faith.

will sometimes tell us this is worth pursuing, even if it wasn't in my original plan. As we consider what types of jobs we would take or where we could potentially work, a sense of openness can be the key to not drawing too many limits on the future.

How open to be in the job-search process is a matter of preference. One job seeker may decide to take any job, just to keep food on the table. Another person might hold off for a job that's closest to their experience. Openness, in other words, must be paired with discernment about what's calling and what's not. Discernment is sort of like decision-making, but discernment concerns larger issues that affect our lives. For instance, we decide where to go for dinner; we discern whether to move to a new place for a job. When we try to discern about what work to pursue, we are doing more than deciding whether to take a certain job. We are also asking what God wants for our lives.

Here is a tool for the discernment process. St. Ignatius developed a prayer called the Examen. In essence, the process provides a way to "examine" our lives on a day-to-day basis and get a sense of where God may be leading us. Each evening, for a month, we can look back over our day and write down two moments from the day: (1) a time during the day when we felt joyful and (2) a time during the day when we struggled. The point of the Examen is to recognize that God works through both our good times and our bad times. After a month of recording those moments from each day, we have enough data to see patterns in our lives. For instance, a software engineer may realize that her worst moment each day is going to work and may become motivated to try a more life-giving career. A dad may figure out that walking his kids to school each morning is the highlight of his day and commit to looking for a part-time job in order to keep up this practice.

Openness means being curious about what God might be up to in the universe and being willing to take a risk in the name of faith.

Examen Prayer

The Daily Examen is a technique of prayerful reflection on the events of the day in order to detect God's presence and discern his direction for us. The Examen is an ancient practice in the church that can help us see God's hand at work in our whole experience.

How Do I Pray an Examen Prayer?

1. Breathe in God's unconditional love through deep breaths.

2. Place your hand on your heart and recall a moment of the day about which you feel the most thankful. This moment is called the consolation. Recall the specialness of that moment.

3. Recall a moment of the day about which you feel the least grateful. This moment is called the desolation. Ask God to be with you in remembering that moment and learning from whatever happened at that time of the day.

4. Give thanks for the way that God works through both our consolation and desolation.

The Examen Prayer can be a simple yet powerful way to pray with our children. At the end of the day, we can gather as a family to remember each person's happiest and saddest time of the day. Hearing about each other's high and low moments shows respect for children and adults alike and draws us closer through prayer.

P—Puzzles

Do you happen to like Sudoku puzzles or crossword puzzles? If so, you are in luck. The creative art of puzzling comes in handy when searching for a job. Faith is often puzzling, isn't it? Our rational knowledge doesn't necessarily solve the puzzles of how to be faithful and trusting in hard times. Instead we must amass our little parcels of belief to work together with other people to find hope. Somehow God grace-fully works with us to interconnect our separate answers into a larger, trickier picture of God at work.

Here are a couple of clues for solving crosswords from a consummate puzzler:

1. Short-term solutions lead to longer answers.

> Short-term solutions lead to longer answers.
>
> Guessing and peeking have their place.
>
> Never stop trying.

In most crossword puzzles there are three to four long answers that stretch all the way across the puzzle. The long answers usually follow a theme that is foreshadowed in the puzzle title. If it's the *New York Times* Sunday puzzle the theme is likely to include tricky puns or some surprising twist. At any rate, you can't usually start by trying to figure out those long answers. Instead you go with the short answers, and by solving enough of those, you can often decipher the longer mysteries. The same proves true for job seeking. Consistently sending out resumés and applications eventually leads to a larger answer, a job!

2. Guessing and peeking have their place.

After hours of work on a puzzle, that magical moment comes when you give yourself permission to just start guessing. What have you got to lose, after all? Maybe you begin to trust that you might know more than you think you do, or you realize that a mistake can be erased. So what the heck! You turn to the answer pages at the back of the puzzle magazine to look up a particularly obscure answer, like the winner of a 1964 Academy Award. During job loss, we finally begin to trust God enough to risk taking a chance on change, and embrace new ways of thinking.

God's presence—right in the middle of the puzzle—is just waiting for us to realize we know it and want to use it to tackle job loss.

3. Never stop trying.

Sometimes, if we're working on a big Sunday puzzle, we can leave the puzzle for a few days and come back to it with fresh eyes. Suddenly the answers jump out at us. Here's how the phenomenon happens. Before we even begin to read the clues again, we can look at a partially filled-in word, and see what's supposed to be there. This amazing moment can happen only because we just know intuitively how words look and work. The letter Q is almost always followed by a U. C is not followed by G. As people of faith, we also have that underlying sense about how God works. God's presence—right in the middle of the puzzle—is just waiting for us to realize we know it and want to use it to tackle job loss.

Q—Questions/Quiet

You would think that we would be hard-pressed to find spiritual words that start with Q to add to our list of spiritual tools. But in fact, there are two Q words that fit the bill and dovetail effectively in the spiritual life.

The first Q word is *questions*. We need to become expert question-askers at this point. Each day, in order to get what we need, we have questions of everyone. The unemployment benefits specialist, the retooling expert, the babysitter, the landlord, the human-resources office, and the moving-van company, to name a few. Sometimes there's no one to ask, but we still need to clarify our questions so we can find them in a Frequently Asked Questions list on a website.

We also need to become adept question answerers. Here's what I mean: We will have to answer the question "What kind of job are you looking for?" by writing a succinct purpose statement on our resumé. In interviews we will also need to be prepared to answer multiple questions about our experience and references, all of which basically boil down to "Why should we hire you?"

The question categories we have named so far have to do with practical matters that help us navigate the tasks of unemployment and reemployment. There are also spiritual questions rumbling around in our soul, and we can dare to ask those as well. We can

When has God answered your questions?

Where are your favorite quiet places?

Amidst the noise of our society and the added clamor of our worries, we need to find a quiet place each day and listen for God.

take those BIG questions to God, and we should! God is not afraid to hear us call out. Why did I lose my job? What are we going to do? When will you help us, O God? Where is the justice here? How will our family weather this storm? Those questions are really prayers, and addressing them to God means we are praying in one of the most fervent and effective ways of all. We find some peace in sharing our deepest hurts and admitting that we absolutely need God.

Undoubtedly you've already thought of the obvious problem with questioning God. How do we question God when God doesn't seem to answer back? This is where the second Q in our list comes in, *quiet*. Amidst the noise of our society and the added clamor of our worries, we need to find a quiet place each day and listen for God. God's answers can often come as hints and whispers—which require quiet to hear.

R—Reading

In the Q section, we talked about asking questions of God. The experience of questioning God may seem very sacrilegious to some of us. There are models of faith, such as Dietrich Bonhoeffer and Nelson Mandela, who have reassured us that calling out to God for answers is part of the process of discipleship. In their years of captivity for faithful causes, they had plenty of questions for God. We can read their work and find inspiration from these lions of faith.

And that's just the beginning. There are many other writers worth reading as we try to keep our spirits buoyed and our faith fed. Some spiritual writers deal specifically with job loss and the theology of work.

S—Service

My mom was undoubtedly right when she recommended that I help others as an antidote to self-pity. I didn't appreciate her advice

Here are a few book and blog recommendations:

Books

Care of the Soul by Thomas Moore

A Life at Work by Thomas Moore

The War of Art by Steven Pressfield

The Quotidian Mysteries by Kathleen Norris

Acedia and Me by Kathleen Norris

Work: How to Find Joy and Meaning in Each Hour of the Day by Thich Nhat Hanh

Called to Question by Sister Joan Chittister

The Gift of Years by Sister Joan Chittister

Discernment: Reading the Signs of Daily Life by Henri Nouwen

Take and Read: Spiritual Reading by Eugene Peterson

Run with the Horses by Eugene Peterson

Spirituality of the Psalms by Walter Brueggemann

A Way Other Than Our Own by Walter Brueggemann

Blogs and Sermons

On Being with Krista Tippett (onbeing.org)

Center for Faith and Work (www.gospelinlife.com/center-for-faith-and-work)

www.patheos.com

Holy Rover (patheos.com/blogs/holyrover)

spiritualityandpractice.com

Ignatianspirituality.com

www.nadiabolzweber.com

lectionarylab.com

www.homeboyindustries.org/fatherg

Institute for Faith, Work, and Economics (tifwe.org/blog)

at the time, and I still don't recommend "other pity" as a detour around self-pity. But she was right in the idea that we can gain lots of perspective on our issues by engaging in bigger worlds and helping others.

A day of physical labor volunteering for a home-building nonprofit can really refresh our minds. The day can also boost our spirits, knowing that we are part of a solution, rather than merely the victim of a problem.

Years ago, while visiting church partners in Mexico, our group was invited to eat lunch with our hosts. We felt very humbled, recognizing that our lunch included the only tortillas our hosts could afford for the day. That experience reminded me of the enormous blessings inherent in service. We often find out how much we are being served when we say yes to serving others.

> We often find out how much we are being served when we say yes to serving others.

T—Tears

While mastering the skill of reading, schoolchildren learn about homonyms—words that are spelled or sound the same, but have different meanings. As an example, new readers must distinguish between tears (a sign of crying) and tears (rips in paper or clothing). One new reader solved the problem for her classmates by pointing out that tears (rips) can lead to tears (a sign of sadness). Her words couldn't be truer for us when we face job loss and respond with an expression of grief. Our lives feel suddenly torn apart, and as we survey the ripped fabric of our existence, all we can do is cry.

> Tears are beautiful spiritual gifts.

If we're lucky, that is. For tears are beautiful spiritual gifts. There's nothing like cleaning out our tear ducts to also give our souls a good rinse. After a good cry, we somehow feel like children again.

How are tears a gift from God?

How has the fabric of your life been torn apart by job loss?

That's good, because as children we may have been more sure of God's presence, more trusting of the mystery of faith. Most kids, when they learn about faith at an early age, embrace the Bible stories and believe that Jesus does love them. Later, when they become upper-elementary students and discover their scientific mind, these kids face a quandary. How can God be everywhere (as it says in the Bible), and yet that not be possible from a factual perspective? Eventually kids integrate their faith perspective with their factual perspective, balancing what they see and what they don't see.

Returning to a less jaded sense of faith can open our tear-stained eyes to what we forgot to see—God at work in our lives, even in challenging moments. Especially at challenging moments.

U—Understanding

The stress of losing a job can be devastating to a family. That's because everyone's discomfort merges to create a fever pitch. When we are all on edge, the least little thing can cause us to overreact in anger and mistrust. The greatest gift we can give one another at times like this is understanding. Yet this gift seems so hard to enact.

Giving one another space helps us to appreciate one another's plight. When we are all stuck at home, without our old workplace outlets, we can really step on one another's toes. Agreeing on some compromises and space sharing helps, particularly if there is childcare involved. We can allot responsibilities during certain times of the day so that the other person can go to the library or take a walk.

Create some ground rules. Writing them out on a sheet of paper and posting it can help. For instance, we can write things like "During this time of change, we will make an extra effort to compromise. We will all try to learn to do new things for ourselves." When we recognize that we are going through a new and trying experience, we can attempt to consciously deal with the tribulation,

The greatest gift we can give one another at times like this is understanding.

rather than deny the changes and be surprised when everyone falls apart. We can call on understanding grandparents, counselors, and trusted neighbors to contribute errands, childcare, and the perspective of age.

Understanding can be easier to maintain at home if we have other avenues where we can express our range of emotions. Telling a friend or confidante about our feelings of fear and anger can help us keep from constantly taking out those things on the person who lost the job. If children are involved, one of the lasting lessons they can learn about the resilience of marriage is watching their parents be decent to one another through a trying time.

Speaking of children, they also need a heavy dose of understanding during unemployment. They may have lost precious parts of their lives as changes were made—like losing a familiar room, classmates, and routines. Remembering that parents are typically kids' main source of security encourages us to keep providing our little ones with time, love, and understanding.

V—Vocation

In spite of facing frightening unknowns and navigating the shoals of change, job loss can also lead to relief. Particularly when we are forced out of a safe job that never really felt like what we wanted to do "deep down." We are talking about vocation here. Vocation means a summons to a particular kind of work. We've heard the word *summons* used in a legal sense, when one receives a "summons" to go to court. In other words, there is no choice but to go. The word *vocation* implies a sort of deep gravitational pull to do something. We simply must pursue a vocation, because that's who we are.

> Our sustenance remains a gift from God, but we are invited into a deeper gift—the gift of participation in the life-giving work of God through our vocation.

What reflections do you have about Luther's ideas on vocation?

Which of your jobs has felt most clearly like what God intended for you?

We have included Vocation on the list of spiritual tools, because this word has a religious connotation. Vocation is also used as a word to name a sacred call to the spiritual life.

Martin Luther wrote, "God gives food, not as God did when God gave manna from heaven, but through labor, when we diligently perform the work of our calling" (Martin Luther, *Lectures on Genesis*, AE 3:273–74).

Before Martin Luther began teaching about vocation, the medieval church differentiated between common work and "vocation." The church believed that all people had to work, but only certain workers fulfilled a sacred vocation or calling. While farmers, merchants, and workers in the home went about the daily business of their lives, priests, nuns, and monks were doing "God's work." Their jobs were viewed as sacred callings that made them closer to God (ELCA World Hunger Lenten Study 2017 on Lutheran Economic Ethics).

In one of his most important reforms, Martin Luther did more than just break down this barrier; he reversed it! Ordinary work, he believed, was ordained in the Bible, while life as a monk or a nun was not. In his writings on Genesis, Luther wrote:

> Thus every person surely has a calling. While attending to it, he serves God. . . . When a maid milks the cows or a hired man hoes the field—provided they are believers, namely, that they conclude that this kind of life is pleasing to God and was instituted by God— they serve God more than all the monks and nuns, who cannot be sure about their kind of life.[2]

Not only did Luther believe that every person has a sacred calling or vocation, he believed that doing this work was "pleasing to God [and] instituted by God." German theologian Gustaf Wingren wrote that Luther believed "There is a direct connection between God's work in creation and [God's] work in [humans' daily jobs]."[3] In other words, God is with us in our job hunt, hoping that we will find the work God created us to do.

W—Writing

Writing constitutes a holy endeavor, for in expressing ourselves we tap into our creativity and discover a reliable method for responding to a deep sense of healing. Writing can take many forms. We may survive the pain of job loss by writing letters to ourselves each day as a source of encouragement. We may also simply journal our experience as a way of sorting out the myriad feelings and events.

And we don't always have to write alone. We can write about much more than the pain of job loss and the conundrum of job searching in an unemployment support group. At any given meeting, members may also write memories of their own family work histories and dreams for the future. A leader suggests a simple writing exercise, and participants spend a short time writing their truth. If people want to read aloud, that's helpful. But the writing itself is also a powerful tool for enhancing organization and self-awareness. When someone does read aloud, the other members of the group simply listen and perhaps just say what they remembered. Such a writing experience is not a critique group, nor is it a therapy group. Writing merely serves as a healing medium to get what's inside out.

While writing may sound very basic, we shouldn't underestimate its influence in one's life. Scientific studies have proven that writing can improve psychological health, lead to greater insight and self-reflection, and promote empathy.[4] When we go through a challenging situation in our lives, such as job loss, our souls tend to be overflowing with a mass of feelings, questions, and reflections. Writing on a regular basis, alone or with others, can give us a chance to empty out our souls and see what's there.

X—X-Ray Vision

The skill of seeing what's not yet there—that skill describes the life of faith, doesn't it? Seeing what's not yet there also describes imagining a future that's better than the present. This may sound very naïve, especially on those days when rejection emails arrive.

> Writing constitutes a holy endeavor, for in expressing ourselves we tap into our creativity and discover a reliable method for responding to a deep sense of healing.

> Writing on a regular basis, alone or with others, can give us a chance to empty out our souls and see what's there.

> What do you imagine when you dream of a hopeful employment future?
>
> How do you share your sense of imagination with friends and family?

Or when no word arrives and we are left to wonder if our hard work applying for jobs meant nothing. Amidst those crushing feelings, how in the world can we see more than what's there?

It's brutally hard sometimes, but we can still use our imaginations. After all, companies can dismiss us from our jobs, employers can ignore our pleas for new work, and society can doubt our potential. But no one can remove our sense of imagination. We can cling to that shred of faith to keep a vision of what we're hoping for and working for. Imagining what is not there sounds kind of silly, doesn't it? And that's perfect—because having a good imagination goes hand in hand with having a good sense of humor. At the end of the day, regaining the ability to laugh at ourselves or the experience—even a little—can keep us sane.

Y—Yelling in the Car

For those days when seeing beyond the present reality and chuckling as we imagine a better tomorrow seem impossible, we can go yell in the car. What?! That's right—go yell in the car. There are four rules:

1. Go alone.
2. Go park in a safe, unfamiliar, sparsely populated area to do the yelling.
3. Yell only at God.
4. Make sure the windows are rolled up.

Seriously! Tell God exactly how you feel about all that's happened. Get it off your chest. God can definitely take it. And you will actually show God that you take God seriously by reminding

Tell God exactly how you feel about all that's happened. Get it off your chest. God can definitely take it.

God of who you are and what you can do. You know what they say about prayer—that prayer changes the one praying as much as it changes God. Getting all that emotion out can result in an enormous sense of peace for us. The pot boiled over (in a safe environment) and we got to take the problem to God in a big, real, I'm-not-kidding way. Just don't forget the four rules.

Z—Zing

After a whole alphabet of spiritual strategies to deal with the topic of job loss, we are so lucky to have a Z word, *Zing*, that implies celebration. The end of our job hunt does finally arrive, our worries and panic do eventually fade, and our children do get to go back to worrying about things like where to get the best Halloween candy. Answers really do arrive, sometimes after long waits and sometimes through serendipitous encounters.

How do you like to celebrate good news with your family?

Who are the people who have helped you and would love to hear about your new job? How could you let them know?

When we arrive at those glorious finales, those moments of zing, celebration is as important as all the other spiritual tools combined. Allowing ourselves to feel the relief, rest in a more deeply held faith, and say thanks for God's presence through it all—that's Zing!

Resources

Worden, J. William. *Grief Counseling and Grief Therapy*. New York: Spring, 2009.

- A book that explains the tasks of grief.

Spiritual Directors International. sdiworld.org.

- A respected website where you can find a spiritual director who works near where you live.

Christ in Our Home. Augsburg Fortress. https://tinyurl.com/y9j6p3ru.

- The Lutheran publishing house's quarterly devotional. Other denominations publish their own devotionals.

NPR Tiny Desk Concerts. https://tinyurl.com/y72dkdvy.

- Offers a chance to hear new and old music in an intimate setting.

McGirr, Michael. *Snooze: The Lost Art of Sleep.* New York: Pegasus, 2017.

- A book about the topic of sleep in history, literature, and medicine. McGirr is a former Jesuit priest with many wise and witty reflections to share.

Amherst Writers & Artists. amherstwriters.org.

- Offers training in leading writing groups and can help you find writing workshops in your area.

Answers really do arrive, sometimes after long waits and sometimes through serendipitous encounters.

4

Ten Questions to Help You Get from Here (No Job) to There (Job)

HAVE YOU ever stood at the edge of a canyon and gazed out at the vast emptiness between where you stand and the other side? Sometimes we get that same sense of endless space between us and the achievement of a large goal, like finding a job. We can be very clear about what we want. We can even see the other side in the distance. But getting there still seems to be an arduous, perplexing journey.

In this chapter, we're going to outline the steps of getting from one side of the canyon to the other (in other words, from no job to a job) by using some proven coaching strategies. Coaches employ a variety of methods to help their clients. One of the simplest methods works like this. First, identify a goal you have for yourself and write this down. (In this case, employment.)

Goal: Employment

Next, identify where you are now and add that word to the diagram.

Goal: Employment

Current Situation: Unemployed

You are almost finished with the diagram. There's one more step. Between the two things you've written, identify steps that help you get from where you are to where you want to be. For example, update resumé, find a job coach, and apply for positions.

Goal: Employment

Step 3

Step 2

Step 1

Current Situation: Unemployed

We have a plan and we can picture the plan.

The diagram looks organized, doesn't it? Undoubtedly this picture seems much clearer than the muddle in our heads. But of course, the process isn't quite as simple as the diagram implies. As we identify and fulfill the necessary steps of finding a job, we can expect to do a lot of circling back, getting stuck, and figuring out the next step. Nevertheless, using this simple coaching plan as a visual aid can ease our anxiety.

At the beginning of "getting from here to there," we have feelings, skills, ideas, and dreams locked inside us. We need to pay attention to these inner clues because they offer more pictures of the future. The idea is to express the ideas rumbling around inside us so we can begin using them to move forward. We can express our ideas by writing outlines on whiteboards, putting up lists on the walls, adding file folders for keeping things sorted out, and piling business cards where we can see them on our desk. Or maybe you don't work on a desk. No problem. Just find a clear file box in which you can temporarily store your find-a-job materials. The clear box helps them from getting buried and forgotten.

You might be saying, "But I do all this on my computer." That's fine. The same underlying principles apply:

1. Make a diagram of your goal, your current condition, and potential steps in between.
2. Create additional charts and lists to define and monitor your progress.

3. Review your materials frequently to ensure that things don't get hidden or lost.

4. Create a job folder on your computer desktop so you can easily access your materials.

All of this organizing at the start of a job search is a lot like cleaning out our cupboards and fridge before starting a healthier eating plan. When we create new systems, we stand a better chance of improving our habits (and not being at the mercy of a stash of chocolate bars).

Even if we work electronically, having a whiteboard gives us a place to brainstorm and the freedom to erase and replace ideas as the job searching proceeds. There's something about colorful, smooth whiteboard markers that helps us have fun and get started.

Getting started each day to make progress on our job search can be one of our biggest challenges of all. Particularly when the task is potentially daunting, like job searching, avoidance can be a natural response and even a stubborn habit. We are likely to hone our resistance skills until we're very adept at task avoidance. But when our livelihood and the welfare of others is at stake, we can usually boot ourselves into a small starting step.

Someone once asked a world-renowned concert pianist, "How do you practice for hours each day in order to play so well?" His answer came as a surprise. The pianist responded that he did not, in fact, practice for hours each day. Instead, he practiced for five minutes. What? How could this be? The pianist explained: "The hardest thing for me is to get started. So I set a timer for five minutes and practice for that long. After five minutes of practicing, I'm fine to continue. So then I can play for hours."

For the remainder of this chapter, we will be working on the steps that fall in between your current situation (no job) and your goal (a job). It sounds so tidy, doesn't it? Just name the steps and walk the staircase from one task to another. So why, we ask, does it feel like a scary, yawning chasm to get from here to there? There are many reasons.

Even if we work electronically, having a whiteboard gives us a place to brainstorm and the freedom to erase and replace ideas as the job searching proceeds. There's something about colorful, smooth whiteboard markers that helps us have fun and get started.

Years ago, I somehow got the notion in my head to attempt a ropes-course challenge with a coworker. The whole idea was rather far-fetched, because I'm afraid of heights and my coworker and I did not always work well together. The ropes were arranged in a sort of vertical ladder with horizontal wooden rungs every six feet or so. One person had to balance her side of the rung while the other person pulled herself up to the next rung.

When we started the challenge, I gazed up to the very high ceiling above where we were supposed to finish and confessed, "I really don't think I can get there." My coworker kept her cool. She merely suggested, "Why don't we just try to get to the next rung?" That's what we did, very slowly. My arms and legs were shaking, but she helped me and I helped her. As we rested on each subsequent rung, getting to the next one seemed possible.

She merely suggested, "Why don't we just try to get to the next rung?"

You know the rest of the story. We made it to the top, rung by rung. I gained enormous respect for my coworker. When we reached the top, our spotters helped us rappel down from the ceiling and we celebrated. A scary journey gets accomplished little by little, with others to partner with us. The trek becomes less scary when we manage our expectations and accept support along the way.

Throughout my rope-ladder experience, a central doubt rang in my head: Can I do this? We all have many questions filling our minds during a job search process. Here are ten common questions we ask, with ideas to help us get to the next rung.

Why does starting the job-hunt process feel so overwhelming?

This entire book has been an attempt to answer that question. Job loss touches on very deep and tender emotions, such as shame, panic, loss, and disappointment. We may feel several of these powerful feelings at once and feel drowned by their intensity.

The process of looking for a job is overwhelming, therefore, because of the magnitude of our feelings and the complexity of this thing called work. For some of us, the idea of starting to search for new employment feels nearly impossible because we are still wrapped up in grieving the loss of our old job and life. Grieving is the key word here. It can take time to feel the sadness, fear, and displacement of job loss. Almost like the way we feel when someone dies or a significant relationship ends. When we leave, we grieve. Grief can manifest itself as wanting to sleep all day, testiness, crying, and resistance to change. When we are in the depths of grief, we can scarcely see our way out. That's why it's so helpful to find companions to walk with us, including folks who have grieved losses and know that we do indeed come out in a different place.

Grief can mean something a little different for each person, but basically it means that we're all human and change rattles our world. When someone tells us to "do our grief work," that means we need to acknowledge our loss, express our feelings in an intentional way such as writing, be patient with ourselves during the time grief takes, seek help in many forms, and trust that healing arrives eventually and will bring new life.

So unresolved grief constitutes one reason that starting a job search feels so overwhelming. Another reason confronts us every time we go to a job site or think of working on our resumé. We simply don't think we possess the knowledge to pull off a job finding process. Too many questions attack us at once, and we feel uneducated about how to power through. Let's look at a few of those questions right now, in order to lessen that sense of being overwhelmed:

How do I write or update my resumé?

Without hard data to back up this theory, I would hypothesize that most people would prefer going to the dentist to writing a resumé. At least in the dentist chair, the fear and discomfort are confined to a few hours. We can let the anxiety of resumé writing bleed over days and weeks. It's so hard to master this essential document.

For some of us, the idea of starting to search for new employment feels nearly impossible because we are still wrapped up in grieving the loss of our old job and life.

Resumés are a lot like fashion; they reflect trends that come and go. We may hear conflicting pieces of advice, such as the following: *Be sure the resumé fits on a page. Don't worry about multiple pages. Be detailed about your experiences. Simply summarize your experiences. Include a picture. Don't include a picture.* We need to make multiple decisions as we craft our resumé.

Because resumé styles vary and constantly evolve, smart job searchers look for trusted sources or a person currently schooled in the employment search process. How do we decide whether a source is trustworthy? We can stick with academic sites and familiar names, or ask friends for recommendations. There are many resources, help lines, and tutorials available online. Look for sources or people who are familiar with their line of work. What's expected in one world might be very different from what's expected in another. If that works for you, great. But what about those of us who do better with an actual person helping us? We can acknowledge that preference, and search and pray for such helpers. Employment services, coaches, and outplacement representatives can be great places to start. We can connect with people in a variety of ways, from simply typing "free resumé help" into Google to asking to put a note in our church newsletter requesting help. Often just having someone sit with us during the resumé-writing task can give us exactly the moral support we need.

In addition to preparing our resumé, another step is to create or update our electronic resumé on appropriate employment-oriented social-networking services. Some potential employers will expect you to have a current summary of your work on one of these sites. The sites offer templates and options from basic to elaborate for describing and showing your accomplishments. Even people who are currently employed often have the goal of updating or revising their online information. Therefore, we can gather a group of friends for a two-hour social-networking boot camp during which we all accomplish a desired outcome and offer each other feedback and expertise.

> Because resumé styles vary and constantly evolve, smart job searchers look for trusted sources or a person currently schooled in the employment search process.

To further demystify the resumé-writing step, consider the word *resume*, which is the same as *resumé*, minus the accent mark. The official document, which we stress over, has a clear goal—to help us resume our work life. Each section of the document—references, education, and past employment—is aimed at restarting our idled engines. Writing those pieces, while sometimes tedious, keeps us focused on a better future.

In order to resume what we sidelined—whether through our own volition (for example, we left the workplace to stay home with our kids) or through company downsizing or closing—we need to communicate about ourselves in writing. Read some resumés online or in business manuals. Imagine yourself on the other side of the hiring desk. Notice how each resumé portrays a particular style, tone, and picture of a person. You might use this activity to help clarify how you want to portray yourself. Ask a friend or acquaintance to read your resumé draft and offer feedback on how you sound in words. Be specific about what you are asking of your reader. Do you want a general impression or another set of eyes to check for typos and other mistakes?

Earlier we mentioned that trends in resumés come and go, like skirt lengths. However, some things never change:

1. Resumés should be meticulously checked to be sure there are no errors whatsoever. Employers equate a sloppy resumé with a worker who would not go the extra mile to get things right.[1]
2. Resumés should be honest. Of course.
3. Resumés should highlight transferable skills. Smart employers recognize the multitasking abilities of a parent who stayed home to raise kids and volunteered to help run school programs, sports, and other activities. Astute hirers realize the sacrifices potential employees have made to care for aging parents. The skills, values, and discipline these potential employees offer can bring enormous strength to a workplace. Figuring out how to word your beyond-the-workplace skills can be a stimulating

> Employers equate a sloppy resumé with a worker who would not go the extra mile to get things right.

writing challenge. And it's the best kind of writing challenge—
one with a purpose.

Why am I having nightmares about usernames and passwords?

In our increasingly automated culture, job hunts are fraught with
electronic steps. Before we can download our resumés and cover
letter for particular jobs, we have to get through cyberspace
doorways. That means registering in a variety of corporate and
human resources systems. This can be time-consuming and
frustrating, even for young job seekers. The practice feels so
impersonal and devoid of connection. But there you have it.

We can waste energy feeling frustrated by the way portals work or
use that energy to apply and gain confidence each time we fulfill
the drill. Not that electronic application processes are all bad! In
many cases, once we complete and submit our materials, we can
track the status of our application online. The updates can increase
accountability and help us manage our stress about the unknown.

Even if you possess an infinite number of technology-loving brain
cells, do yourself a big favor by writing down all your usernames
and passwords to stay organized. If you prefer to work on a
computer, create a spreadsheet to store your information.

Now that we have made some peace with electronic application
processes as a necessary stage in the job hunt process, let's recall
something very old school: most jobs come out of very personal
connections, rather than resumés launched into cyberspace. For
instance, Joe got his job through his next-door neighbor, who works
in the computer industry. Cate was able to step in as a house sitter
when her friend recommended her.

When looking for a job, the smartest investment we can make is
to tap our networks. These folks know many more work fields and
people. They can help us get in actual doors, not just virtual doors,
for interviews and auditions.

Most jobs come
out of very personal
connections, rather than
resumés launched into
cyberspace.

God loves us, whether or not we remember our password.

Who's in our network? To answer this question, think about a typical week in your life and all the people you encounter, such as Facebook friends, yoga classmates, church members, PTA colleagues, parents, college alumni, grocery store clerks, neighbors, carpool parents, family, sports buddies, fellow volunteers, and former coworkers. All of us are connected to more groups than we can even imagine. The biggest thing that keeps us from contacting these people may be our wounded pride. Try to swallow that pride and reach out, knowing that the vast majority of people want nothing more than the opportunity to help someone else.

On those days when the job search becomes all too much, and all those usernames and passwords get into a giant knot in our brain and soul—turn to Isaiah 43:1, "I have called you by name." Relish this ancient truth that God loves us, whether or not we remember our password. The username God chose for us is Child of God. This title encompasses humility, forgiveness, second chances, justice, and empowerment.

What are cover letters supposed to cover?

Just for a moment, pretend you work as a woodworker who makes beautiful furniture. Imagine yourself in your workshop, surveying your tools and products. Now take this imaginary scenario a step further by pretending you need to take an unexpected trip or be admitted to the hospital. You have furniture orders to fill for customers, so you want to hire someone to care for your business. Who are you looking for? Someone who . . .

- Has experience building furniture
- Finishes in a timely manner
- Creates furniture worthy of your company
- Knows the tools
- Works well with you
- Cares about safety
- Can deliver a competent product

- Takes pride in their work
- Focuses on the task at hand

Okay, now that you have in mind who you want to hire, think about going to the mailbox and receiving letters from furniture makers applying for the position. What should their cover letters include? Certainly, information about themselves, including experience. Beyond that, the letters you read from potential employees should include a sense that they truly know and care about the trade of woodworking.

Every job we apply for represents someone's "workshop business" that they are potentially sharing with us. Therefore, when we write a cover letter, we need to keep in mind that "business owner" and their product and remember that an employer expects the same of us, namely to be capable and professional. A well-written cover letter shows that we know about the work itself. Maybe we are writing to a principal responsible for hiring teachers for a school. Or perhaps we hope a construction manager will choose us for the framing crew of a new building. It doesn't matter what situation we seek. In each case someone who is responsible to get work done is looking for solid help to do so. Therefore our cover letter should demonstrate how we can be of assistance to reach the goals of the enterprise. A cover letter speaks primarily of the work needed.

The reason so many of us shy away from cover letters is that we either worry about being overboastful or get tongue-tied about introducing ourselves. Many of us were schooled by our elders to be modest and understated, and to let our deeds speak for themselves. We worry that we are bragging, but the employer needs information about us. To dial down the intimidation factor, visualize yourself meeting a potential employer in person first. What would you do? Of course you would smile warmly, greet that person, and share something about yourself. Okay, so now smile, greet, and share with real words in a letter form.

Some job seekers thrive on the cover-letter creation process. Our daughter, a college business major, loves to write cover letters. Her

A well-written cover letter shows that we know about the work itself.

secrets include picturing a real person reading the letter, thoroughly researching the organization, and approaching each letter as an opportunity to learn to write better (a goal she measures by how many responses her letters generate).

One of the added pressures of writing an effective cover letter is the increasing desperation we may feel when it takes a long time to find a job. All employers have to do is open a desperate cover letter and the fragrance of panic quickly oozes out.

To reclaim our sense of humor and perspective, we can write a very counterintuitive cover letter once in a while, just for our own eyes. In this personal version, we write frankly about all the reasons we don't want this job. We will definitely be able to come up with reasons, and they will help us know that getting this job is not a be all and end all (even if it is).

Singers "cover" other singers' songs, taking what has already been produced and adding a fresh take on old lyrics and tunes. We can do the same by studying others' cover letters, assessing what seems most effective, and using the letters as models for our own letters. Pay attention to cover letter structures that flow naturally, are clearly organized, and communicate professionalism in engaging tones.

The best favor we can do for ourselves is to put in the time writing and rewriting cover letters. Remember when you were back in high school scrambling to finish an essay the night before it was due? In fact, the teacher could read your work and sense exactly how much effort you put into it. The truth is that we can't really hide how much work we put into our writing. Our second drafts read more confidently than our first drafts do. After enduring the discomfort of rewriting and rewriting again, we walk a little taller and write a little more smoothly. This confidence will come in handy in the interview process.

How do I get ready for an interview?

We feel lots of relief when we get an interview. This step demonstrates getting over the initial hurdles of job searching. Hurray! Someone is interested in us. But how do we stay calm and focused, so we can take full advantage of the opportunity?

Prepare

In order to answer that question, I'll start by asking you a question. Have you ever taught Sunday school, led a children's scout troop, or coached kids' soccer? There's an uncanny similarity between teaching kids and participating in a job interview. Namely, if you prepare, you will survive the experience. If you don't prepare, you are dead in the water. If you're not ready, the kids around you will be more than happy to take over your in-charge role, and it won't be pretty.

What does preparation include? Time, first of all. Kids can "smell a rat" of ill-preparedness; so can interviewers. They will know quickly if you cared enough about the job to do your research and come up with appropriate ways to convey your knowledge. So comb those websites to discover what the companies and people who interview you are made of. Make notes summarizing the information. Bothering to take this step will demonstrate that you care, give you a chance to assess your pertinent experience, and enable you to prepare informed questions.

To further the analogy between teaching a group of kids and attending a job interview—both experiences require us to be in the moment and on our toes. When we have prepared adequately, we can feel confident and present during the interview. That includes responding to inquiries, truly listening to questions, and adapting to whatever comes up in the moment.

Breathe

Our brains function best with adequate oxygen, yet most of us deprive our brains of enough air. Breathing exercises can both

When we have prepared adequately, we can feel confident and present during the interview.

provide us with more of the oxygen our brains need to be productive and help calm us down during anxious situations, such as a job interview.

Before you begin the interview, use this calm breathing technique: Breathe in for four counts through your nose; breathe out for eight counts through your mouth. Do this ten times. Try to make seamless transitions between your inhales and exhales by imagining a wave coming in to shore and going back out. You can tailor the breath count for what works best for you, such as two inhales to four exhales, or three inhales to six exhales. Just be sure the exhale is twice as long as the inhale. Try doing this breathing exercise while you are taking a walk; pace your steps to match the breath counts.

Practice

We never know what we will be asked during a job interview. That's what makes the prospect so nerve-wracking. Preparing for the element of surprise becomes easier when we enlist our friends to help us practice answering interview questions, such as:

* Why do you want this job?
* What challenges have you overcome in life?
* What questions do you have for us?
* Why would you be a good fit for our organization?
* How do you deal with conflict at work?
* What are your career goals?
* Tell about a time when you showed leadership.
* What are your strengths and weaknesses?
* How would your former coworkers describe your work style?
* What do you know about our company?

The beauty of enlisting friends for trial runs is that they will think of other questions from their own interview experiences. We all think we have interview answers in our head, but practicing with a friend helps us take the necessary step of articulating our ideas. The practice sessions prove invaluable for maintaining composure when we are under pressure.

The practice sessions prove invaluable for maintaining composure when we are under pressure.

Pray

Enlisting prayer as a "secret weapon" in the interview process may sound a bit irreverent. But there's nothing quite as empowering as praying for the people who will interview us. We're not trying to control them through prayer. Instead, we are humanizing them in our minds by asking God to be with those folks. Undoubtedly employers come into the interview with their own nervousness and unknowns. By calling on God to care for everyone in the room, we are reminded about what we share as human beings trying to carve out a future and care for our loved ones.

And it never hurts to simply pray to get the job, as well as to pray for God's help to endure whatever the outcome.

Maintain Perspective

At least a shred of perspective, anyway! Remember when we talked about writing a just-for-our-eyes cover letter with reasons we did *not* want the job? Same strategy applies here, to a degree. In other words, try not to go into the interview wearing an air of desperation, even if you feel desperate for work. An interview should ideally be about finding a good match between workplace and employee. Landing a job that's not a good fit typically ends in trouble later.

And although jobs may seem very few and far between, there will be more chances in the future if this chance doesn't work out. Can you actually go into an interview thinking that way? Neither can I! But we can at least try. And we can call our mom or a good friend before or after the interview to boost our confidence. Good luck!

Oh, and don't forget . . .

Prepare a thank you with the name and address of your interviewer. You can finish the handwritten note as soon as you complete the interview and drop it in the mail that day. The gesture will be noticed and appreciated.

> One great strategy job seekers use to make good use of their waiting time is volunteering.

How do I fill my time while I wait for a job?

The job search process requires enormous patience. While we can certainly be proactive about researching jobs and submitting applications, the timelines of those on the other side of the desk are beyond our control. Our wait can seem endless and empty, while over in the human-resources department they are swamped with numerous obligations.

One great strategy job seekers use to make good use of their waiting time is volunteering. Volunteering serves several purposes:

- First, volunteering can serve someone's needs.
- Second, volunteering can give us more experience in the field of work to which we are applying for jobs.
- Third, volunteering boosts our confidence. People rarely say no to someone who wants to volunteer.
- Finally, volunteering counts as job experience. When we add our volunteer experience to our resumés, employers take note of our seriousness about working in the profession.

Service projects and volunteering have become obligatory pieces of an electronic resumé. Potential employers want to see that we are willing to give back, because companies increasingly expect that mindset among their workers and support philanthropic efforts as part of their job.

How do I get my family through this hard time?

When we lose a job, we should find out as quickly as possible what sorts of financial and social-service resources are available, through either our old employer or social-service agencies. Taking care of our family's basic human needs is the immediate priority. We may know nothing about the safety net of social services in our community, or we may have relied on this support at an earlier time. In any case, educating ourselves as soon as possible is essential. We need to ask questions and find people who can help our children and us. The hunt for help can prove difficult and perplexing. Still, we must endure for the sake of our families.

Once we secure at least basic help—food, shelter, and safety—there are many other ways to keep the stress lowered for our children and families. The most important thing we can do is to provide some sort of consistency in the lives of our loved ones. Kids will especially feel the uncertainty of job loss. The more their lives are structured by regular meals, bedtimes, parent interaction, and beloved rituals, the better. As we care for our children, we also care for ourselves. We need to model the consistency we are trying to instill in their disrupted lives. So we choose routines, rather than randomness.

At the beginning of this book, I spoke of how our family turned to prayer on the first day of unemployment (and every subsequent day). In a way, it seemed like there was no other place to turn. And thank goodness! For our kids to witness turning to our faith in a crisis is to teach them one of the most important lessons they could learn for their lives—God cares!

Mealtime or bedtime prayers provide a perfect entrée into praying for better times ahead for your family. Be sure to include daily prayers of gratitude for all the ways abundance has continued in your lives, even in little ways. "Thanks, God, for Aunt Ann babysitting. Thanks for Dad going back to school." Even though it can be scary to picture yourself in their shoes, pray for families in more difficult straits than your own. You will find compassion for others you may not have felt in the same way before.

During the experience of job loss, we adults have to talk about many new things, such as money decisions, stopgap plans, and resource possibilities. The stress can build and build, particularly because there are so many unknowns. If possible, protect your kids from these conversations. They are feeling shaky enough without being in the middle of tense interactions between their parents. Take a walk or ask a friend to watch your kids so you can go and talk or plan.

> The most important thing we can do is to provide some sort of consistency in the lives of our loved ones.

> Give sons and daughters of every age the space and time to ask questions and express their feelings. Just listen and don't promise quick fixes. They mostly want to know that you are there for them.

That said, it would also be unrealistic to think that we can protect our youngsters from all the sadness, fear, or change of job loss. It's good to come up with some age-appropriate phrases to repeat to them each day. "Mommy's finding a new job," would work for young children. "The economy took a downturn," is more appropriate for older kids to understand. Give sons and daughters of every age the space and time to ask questions and express their feelings. Just listen and don't promise quick fixes. They mostly want to know that you are there for them. Provide lots of hugs, I love you's, and prayers for your kids. They need you!

Take advantage of any community resources for kids whose families are facing job loss and connect your children with professional counselors if they need extra support. Kids serve as the barometers of family health; take care of them to ensure that all of you find stability.

One way to empower kids and teens, and calm their frazzled nerves, is to come up with jobs for them around your home. Even though paid employment may be at premium, there's always plenty of work to do. Invite family members to help out in new ways at home to share the load.

Be sure to lighten up in heavy times. Playgrounds, parks, and beaches can offer an escape from the dreariness of home when necessary. Job loss can even lead to new routines of being outside and playing together. Speaking of play, kids love to use their imaginations and can dream up all kinds of ideas about the best job they would like to give their parent. Their hope can be contagious.

We may be tempted to isolate our families from old friends or neighbors. This is only natural. We feel strange about our circumstances and worry that they won't understand or will pity us. Find at least a few friends and family members with whom you can be real and who you know won't judge you or make you feel worse about the situation. Hang around with those folks. They will learn from you, and in the future you can be that safe family for them or someone else. Interactions with others can help your kids feel

Find at least a few friends and family members with whom you can be real and who you know won't judge you or make you feel worse about the situation.

like normal life continues. Also, don't forget to inform your kids' teachers and leaders about what your children are going through at home if the job search stretches on. These leaders can pay special attention to be sure your kids are doing okay.

Finally, when the new job comes through (and it will!), remember to celebrate as a family. You are bonded in a new way through the experience. Now you get to be relieved together, each of you grasping the thrill of employment in a way that others who haven't faced the trauma can't. This is what being a family is all about—going through life's downs, and ups, together. Our children will undoubtedly face job losses and changes sometime during their own employment careers. We are showing them life skills they will need someday.

How can my church help?

Churches can provide a wide variety of resources and programs to help members dealing with job loss.

- *Spiritual Connections*—Pastors and spiritual directors can offer their listening skills to members who have lost their jobs. There's nothing like pouring out our heart to a trusted leader and praying together over a heartache. We can expect your pastor or spiritual director to listen as we articulate your feelings, worries, and ideas. A leader should be able to point us to community resources and be available to pray with us.
- *Support Groups*—Particularly in times when the economy leaves many folks jobless, churches can gather people together to talk to one another and collaborate on ideas for job searching. Having a community of people of faith who truly understand our situation can lift our spirits when we previously felt isolated. For instance, getting parents together to talk about how they are coping can be especially comforting.

Support groups follow different formats. One of the simplest and most respectful formats involves setting a timer for five to ten

Having a community of people of faith who truly understand our situation can lift our spirits when we previously felt isolated.

minutes and allowing one person to use that time to tell about how they are coping with joblessness. Everyone else just listens. After the time's up, there's a moment of silence. This method prevents support group members from interrupting one another and trying to "fix" each other's problems. At other times support groups follow a more interactive format. A skilled leader can ensure that each member of the group gets a chance to talk. As with any groups, setting boundaries and guidelines from the onset helps prevent disrespect among members.

The Kaleidoscope Institute, a think tank for church leaders, has created these respectful communication guidelines:

R = take RESPONSIBILITY for what you say and feel without blaming others.

E = use EMPATHETIC listening.

S = be SENSITIVE to differences in communication styles.

P = PONDER what you hear and feel before you speak.

E = EXAMINE your own assumptions and perceptions.

C = keep CONFIDENTIALITY.

T = TRUST ambiguity because we are *not* here to debate who is right or wrong.

- *Employment Workshops*—Church buildings and meeting rooms provide ideal spaces to host classes on resumé and cover-letter writing, interview strategies, and job-search planning. These classes can be opened to church neighbors and may create new and lasting relationships. Social-service providers or knowledgeable congregation members can teach the classes. The opportunity to teach a class will be especially appreciated by those who are also currently laid off.
- *Social Services*—Many churches house food banks and offer Christmas gift drives that can be a godsend for families going through job loss. Parish nurses may also be available to assess and

support family health. Social workers and counselors affiliated with the church denomination widen the services further.

- **Childcare**—One of the most important services a church can offer is volunteer childcare. Giving parents a break or covering the childcare duties while parents go to interviews and meetings is essential.

Larger Church-Supported Employment Programs

Some churches have created large programs to help those seeking employment. Here are two examples, in case your church wants to explore this option:

Career Transitions Center

Based on the reality that "finding a job is a full-time job," the Career Transitions Center (CTC) of Chicago's mission is to provide professional, emotional, and spiritual support to those seeking a job and looking for meaningful work, and to enhance the employability of incumbent workers. CTC is a volunteer-driven nonprofit organization providing professional assistance to individuals in career and employment transition. CTC also provides outplacement and customized training for incumbent workers.[2]

Center for Faith and Work

Redeemer Presbyterian Church in New York City hosts the Center for Faith and Work (CFW). The center exists to explore and investigate the gospel's unique power to renew hearts, communities, and the world, in and through our day-to-day work. As the cultural renewal arm of Redeemer Presbyterian Church, CTW fosters, shepherds, and empowers the church as it is scattered, living and working out in the world, beyond the walls of any one gathered place of worship. CFW's programming, classes, and events can be characterized by three different areas of emphasis: (1) theological and discipleship training, (2) community formation, and (3) exploring and fostering innovation and imagination in all fields of work.[3]

What other factors can make finding a job even more difficult?

We can easily begin to feel a little paranoid while we wait for a new job, wondering why we are not being hired more quickly. And the truth is, there *are* indeed societal factors that intersect with job loss and can hinder our progress.

The -Isms

Ageism, racism, and sexism continue to thwart humanity's development, so it's no surprise that we discover these injustices during a job search. Each of us will respond to inequity in a unique way, depending on our gifts and temperament. Some of us will choose to focus on things we can control, like our resumé and networking, while attempting to play down factors we can't control, like the "-isms." Others will take advantage of the opportunity to call out unfairness and fight injustice for others and ourselves. After all, when we lose our job and search for another, we don't operate in a vacuum.

The belief systems in our society will affect our chances of landing our next job. But it's important to remember that these flawed systems are not the only thing surrounding us. Our faith communities also surround us, and they care about justice issues, whether or not they always boldly act on their beliefs. Church bodies have drafted social statements about inequity and the "-isms" from a biblical and theological perspective. We may finally become motivated to read these statements when we experience the injustice firsthand.

In the social statement on economic life, the Evangelical Lutheran Church in America (ELCA) affirms that "our identity does not depend on what we do, [but] through our work we should be able to express [our] God-given dignity as persons of integrity, worth, and meaning."[4]

> Ageism, racism, and sexism continue to thwart humanity's development, so it's no surprise that we discover these injustices during a job search.

No matter who we are, our work can be a way we express our deepest values and where our freedom and dignity should be protected from the -isms that destroy relationships.

Homelessness

Think of how hard it is to find a job. Then multiply that difficulty by imagining not having a permanent address or a personal computer. Job loss, potentially compounded by health costs, addiction, and lack of savings, can result in homelessness. Some homelessness is easily visible, like people sleeping on the streets. Other levels of homelessness are hidden in the shadows, such as individuals and families couch-surfing (moving from friend's home to friend's home). The cost to children's sense of security and their ability to continue their education is enormous. Some school systems have adopted a policy of letting children stay enrolled in a home school, even when they frequently move.

Governments, churches, and nonprofit organizations attempt to deal with the issue of homelessness every day, even as the problem balloons. A hundred-year-old Lutheran nonprofit in Seattle, Compass Housing Alliance, provides a post-office box for anyone who needs an address.[5] Thousands of people sign up to receive their mail at Compass, allowing them an opportunity to insert an address on job applications.

Perhaps you are at risk of losing your permanent housing or have had to move already. There are no easy answers beyond searching for social services, relying on the kindness of strangers, and keeping the faith.

New Economies

As we search for employment, we may imagine traditional job scenarios. Meanwhile, the employment field has changed drastically. Employers increasingly hire temporary workers and freelancers. Many jobs are now occupied by workers willing to hold several part-time positions, many of which do not include benefits such as healthcare and retirement. Other workers accept employment for which they are overqualified, specifically to receive healthcare benefits or education subsidies. Bottom line, the work world is changing, and we need to figure out if our expectations match the new realities.

Are we there yet?

Like kids on a long car trip, we may ask that question many times during the weeks and months of joblessness. Are we there yet? Will we ever get there?

One day, we can finally say, yes we are there! We have crossed the empty chasm from one job to another and rest the sweet rest of knowing we are again employed. But we wonder: Will we ever be the same, having experienced job loss? Thankfully, the answer is no. We won't ever be the same. The challenge of getting from here to there has changed us in several meaningful ways:

- Like teenagers who lose a parent to cancer, we can no longer assume that life will proceed according some "expected" way.
- We feel a deeper sense of gratitude for things like a regular paycheck and the morning commute that has enhanced our faith and well-being.
- We may always suffer some post-traumatic stress disorder about job loss, fearing more than a little for our jobs every time we hear of economic downturns or layoffs.
- Ideally, we are more willing to mentor someone else going through job loss and job searching. We "get it" in ways that others do not and can use both our compassion and newfound skills to walk alongside someone else in need.
- We have a new appreciation for God's generosity, which has been revealed through the kindness of friends and strangers toward us.
- Larger issues of job loss and inequity now hold our attention and invite our advocacy in new ways.

But we wonder: Will we ever be the same, having experienced job loss? Thankfully, the answer is no.

- We miss that extra family time that was an unexpected by-product of joblessness.
- We witnessed hope winning the day, even by a slim margin of hope that we mustered each day.

Lessons Learned

I began this book by writing about our family's experience of job loss. We never intended to become experts on the subject, any more than a family touched by Alzheimer's or crime expects to become instantly knowledgeable about a "new normal." Did we find quick wisdom and face each day with grace and a good attitude? I'm afraid not. The trial of job loss was frightening each day and remains an enemy I don't want to meet again. But were we carried by a larger love and delivered to a new place? Absolutely! That's God at work.

None of us is ever the same after any kind of loss. We don't go back to a former life or ever stop remembering the best of that life we lost. But our new life begins to overlap our old life with fresh relationships and opportunities that somehow build on the foundation of the past. After losing his job in the computer industry, my husband pivoted from the field of technology to teaching. Our income decreased, but his joy of life increased, and the sense of fulfillment he has experienced since then has been priceless. Our daughters learned lessons we'll never quite comprehend about the value of money and work, and they have been truly appreciative of the college tuition we provided.

Would I want job loss for anyone else or consent to endure it again? Of course not! But here's the most important spiritual lesson I learned in getting from here to there. What we don't have is exactly what we do have. Here's what I mean by that—when we lose our jobs, we focus on what we don't have: jobs! Of course we want new jobs, and we don't rest until we find them. But what we do have, joblessness, actually includes its own blessings. By struggling with the emptiness and fear of job loss, and by being forced to face all the challenges of caring for our children and finding hope for the future, we discover

God's love, grace, and guidance in a more tangible and trustworthy way. Ideally, we become less judgmental of others and more compassionate in our actions. That's a lesson I hope I never forget.

So the answer to the last question is yes, we get there, even before we arrive at our desired outcome. We get there when we remember that God is there, walking with us to the next moment, the next interview, the next step on a journey of life and faith.

By struggling with the emptiness and fear of job loss, and by being forced to face all the challenges of caring for our children and finding hope for the future, we discover God's love, grace, and guidance in a more tangible and trustworthy way.

Resources

What's Your Grief? whatsyourgrief.com.

- An online resource by mental health professionals with experience helping people grieve many different losses.

"Resumes and Cover Letters." The Career Center at University of California Berkeley. https://tinyurl.com/yctaqk2k.

- A clear description of how to write resumés and cover letters.

Abel, Katy. "When Parents Lose a Job: Talking to Kids about Layoffs." Family Education (blog). https://tinyurl.com/y79efkmx.

- This blogpost by Katy Abel offers additional information for helping your children.

Bunting, Eve. *A Day's Work*. Illustrated by Ronald Himler. New York: Clarion, 1994.

- An award-winning children's book about a young boy helping his grandfather find work as a gardener.

US Equal Employment Opportunity Commission. eeoc.gov.

- Can serve as a resource against discrimination.

Kaleidoscope Institute. kscopeinstitute.org.

- Provides resources to equip church leaders to create sustainable churches and communities.

The Career Transitions Center of Chicago. ctcchicago.org.

• Provides spiritual support for job seekers.

The Center for Faith and Work, New York City. faithandwork.com.

• Explores the intersection of our employment and our belief systems through workshops, newsletters, and conferences.

Notes

Chapter 1: Dealing with Our Feelings about Job Loss

1. Teresa of Ávila, "Let Nothing Disturb You," trans. Henry Wadsworth Longfellow, *Women in Praise of the Sacred: 43 Centuries of Spiritual Poetry by Women*, ed. Jane Hirshfield (New York: HarperPerennial, 1995), 144.

2. "Brief Order for Confession and Forgiveness," *Lutheran Book of Worship* (Minneapolis: Augsburg, 1978), 56.

3. Mother Teresa, "Charity: The Soul of Missionary Activity," *L'Osservatore Romano* (Vatican, April 8, 1991), reprinted on CatholicCulture.org, https://tinyurl.com/y7jfo6yf.

4. *Ein feste Burg ist unser Gott* (1529), trans. Frederic H. Hedge, reported in *Bartlett's Familiar Quotations*, 10th ed., rev. Nathan Haskell Dole (Boston: Little, Brown, 1919).

5. In Edward S. Gleason, *The Prayer-Given Life* (New York: Church Publishing, 2007), 67.

6. From "Evening Prayer," *Evangelical Lutheran Worship* (Minneapolis: Augsburg Fortress, 2006), 317.

7. Trevor Hudson, author of *The Serenity Prayer: A Simple Prayer to Enrich Your Life* (Nashville: Upper Room Books, 2012), has exhaustively researched the origins of this prayer and explains his findings in "The Story Behind the Serenity Prayer," an introduction to his book. He states: "With regard to its authorship, no one can tell for sure who wrote it! . . . What we do know is that its opening lines were used by Reinhold Niebuhr (1892–1971), a Protestant theologian who lectured for several years at the Union Theological Seminary in New York, at the beginning of a chapel address he gave in 1934."

8. "You Are God," World Prayers, https://tinyurl.com/y8mcal4a.

Chapter 2: Thinking about Why We Work

1. Karen Armstrong, "Do unto Others," *The Guardian*, November 14, 2008, https://tinyurl.com/y9wvxbhj.
2. "Guild, Trade Association," Encyclopaedia Britannica (online), https://tinyurl.com/yaemouqp.

Chapter 3: An Alphabet of Spiritual Tools to Cope with Job Loss and Job Search

1. J. William Worden, *Grief Counseling and Grief Therapy* (New York: Springer, 2009), 39.
2. *Luther's Works* 3:128, 321
3. Gustaf Wingren, *Luther on Vocation*, trans. Carl C. Rasmussen (Philadelphia: Muhlenberg, 1954).
4. Celeste Robb-Nicholson, "Writing about Emotions May Ease Stress and Trauma," Harvard Health Publishing, https://tinyurl.com/yac6sa2j.

Chapter 4: Ten Questions to Help You Get from Here (No Job) to There (Job)

1. Aine Cain, "A Woman Who Has Reviewed More than 40,000 Résumés Outlines the 8 Most Annoying Mistakes She Sees," *Business Insider*, March 5, 2017, https://tinyurl.com/ya4wzpwu.
2. "Career Transitions Center of Chicago," Old St. Patrick's Church, https://tinyurl.com/y8b4vktg.
3. The Center for Faith and Work, New York City, faithandwork.com.
4. "Sufficient, Sustainable Livelihood for All," ELCA Social Statement, September 1999, https://tinyurl.com/y7w2ksjb.
5. "Client Services Office," Compass Housing Alliance, https://tinyurl.com/ybfhjk7u.

Bibliography

Armstrong, Karen. "Do unto Others." *The Guardian*, November 14, 2008. https://tinyurl.com/y9wvxbhj.

"Brief Order for Confession and Forgiveness." *Lutheran Book of Worship*. Minneapolis: Augsburg, 1978.

Cain, Aine. "A Woman Who Has Reviewed More than 40,000 Résumés Outlines the 8 Most Annoying Mistakes She Sees." *Business Insider*, March 5, 2017. https://tinyurl.com/ya4wzpwu.

"Career Transitions Center of Chicago." Old St. Patrick's Church. https://tinyurl.com/y8b4vktg.

"Client Services Office." Compass Housing Alliance. https://tinyurl.com/ybfhjk7u.

Ein feste Burg ist unser Gott (1529). Translated by Frederic H. Hedge, reported in *Bartlett's Familiar Quotations*, 10th ed. Revised by Nathan Haskell Dole. Boston: Little, Brown, 1919.

Encyclopaedia Britannica (online). "Guild, Trade Association." https://tinyurl.com/yaemouqp.

"Evening Prayer." *Evangelical Lutheran Worship*. Minneapolis: Augsburg Fortress, 2006.

Gleason, Edward S. *The Prayer-Given Life*. New York: Church Publishing, 2007.

Harvard Health Publishing. "Writing about Emotions May Ease Stress and Trauma." https://tinyurl.com/yac6sa2j.

Hudson, Trevor. *The Serenity Prayer: A Simple Prayer to Enrich Your Life*. Nashville: Upper Room Books, 2012.

Mother Teresa. "Charity: The Soul of Missionary Activity." *L'Osservatore Romano*. Vatican, April 8, 1991. Reprinted on CatholicCulture.org. https://tinyurl.com/y7jfo6yf.

"Sufficient, Sustainable Livelihood for All." ELCA Social Statement, September 1999. https://tinyurl.com/y7w2ksjb.

Teresa of Ávila. "Let Nothing Disturb You." Translated by Henry Wadsworth Longfellow. In *Women in Praise of the Sacred: 43 Centuries of Spiritual Poetry by Women*, edited by Jane Hirshfield. New York: HarperPerennial, 1995.

The Center for Faith and Work, New York City. faithandwork.com.

Worden, J. William. *Grief Counseling and Grief Therapy*. New York: Springer, 2009.

"You Are God." World Prayers. https://tinyurl.com/y8mcal4a.